Life in Miniature

Life in Miniature

A History of Dolls' Houses

Nicola Lisle

PEN & SWORD HISTORY

AN IMPRINT OF PEN & SWORD BOOKS LTD.
YORKSHIRE – PHILADELPHIA

First published in Great Britain in 2020
and reprinted in paperback format in 2021 by
Pen & Sword History
An imprint of
Pen & Sword Books Ltd
Yorkshire - Philadelphia

ISBN 978 1 52679 704 9

Printed and bound by CPI Group (UK) Ltd, Croydon, CR0 4YY

Pen & Sword Books Ltd incorporates the Imprints of Pen & Sword Archaeology, Atlas,
Aviation, Battleground, Discovery, Family History, History, Maritime, Military, Naval,
Politics, Railways, Select, Transport, True Crime, Fiction, Frontline Books, Leo Cooper,
Praetorian Press, Seaforth Publishing, Wharncliffe and White Owl.

For a complete list of Pen & Sword titles please contact

PEN & SWORD BOOKS LIMITED
47 Church Street, Barnsley, South Yorkshire, S70 2AS, England
E-mail: enquiries@pen-and-sword.co.uk
Website: www.pen-and-sword.co.uk

or

PEN AND SWORD BOOKS
1950 Lawrence Rd, Havertown, PA 19083, USA
E-mail: uspen-and-sword@casematepublishers.com
Website: www.penandswordbooks.com

Contents

Acknowledgements

I've had a huge amount of fun researching and writing this book, which has involved visiting dolls' house museums and stately homes up and down the country and finding out more than I realised possible about these wonderful miniatures. As always, I am very grateful to all those who have generously shared their time and expertise with me, including: Emily Toettcher, curator of Amersham Museum; Rebecca Wallis, curator at Uppark; Karthi Abrey and Dr Natalie L. Mann from The Workhouse, Southwell; Janet Boston, curator of Manchester Art Gallery; Brian Newman-Smith, managing director of Bekonscot Model Village; Ed and Emily Paris, former owners of Corfe Castle Model Village, and the current owner Macelio Andrade; Samantha Payne, house steward at Saltram; Donna Williams, house steward at Overbeck's; Susan Gardner, curator at the Museum of Childhood, City of Edinburgh Council; Louise Vincent and Ros Liddington at Wilton House; Marian Barker at Old House Museum, Bakewell; Tessa Blake, house steward at Greys Court; Ellen Turnock, volunteer at Upton House; Kayleigh Edun, education officer at the Charles Dickens Museum; and Dawn Hoskin, curator at Sudbury Hall.

I am grateful to the National Trust for permission to quote from *Days Far Away: Memories of Charles Paget Wade 1883-1956*, compiled and edited by Michael Jessup for the National Trust (National Trust Enterprises Ltd, 1996). I am also grateful to the Museum of Childhood, City of Edinburgh Council, for permission to reproduce quotes by Lena Montgomery (p. 56) and Patrick Murray (pp. 135, 147 and 148).

Thank you to Heather Williams and all the editorial and production team at Pen & Sword Books for all their help and endless patience!

Finally, thanks to my mother, Doreen Pinnell, for proofreading the book and giving helpful feedback; and, as always, to my husband, James, and son, Ben, for all their support and encouragement.

Cover picture credits

All cover pictures © Nicola Lisle.

Front cover: top left and centre, reproduced by kind permission of the Museum of Childhood, City of Edinburgh Council; top right, taken and reproduced by kind permission of the Museum of Cambridge. Main picture reproduced by kind permission of the Tolsey Museum, Burford.

Back cover: Picture reproduced by kind permission of Ilkley Toy Museum.

Inside back flap: Reproduced by kind permission of Worthing Museum and Art Gallery.

Introduction

'One Christmas he returned with an enormous dolls' house ... We fingered and commented on the many apertures, bits of furniture all jumbled together and the sectioned off rooms. Anyone could see it was for me, the only girl in the family, and I cannot remember being more touched by any other one event.'

Aeronwy Thomas: *A Daughter Remembers Dylan* (Merton Books, 2006)

Dolls' houses and their miniature contents have fascinated, delighted and inspired people, from ordinary folk to royalty and the aristocracy, since at least the sixteenth century.

We think of dolls' houses now as toys, but originally they were showpieces for adults to display their collections of valuable, finely crafted miniatures that boasted of their wealth and social status. It was not until the late eighteenth century that dolls' houses started to become playthings for children, but they were still very much the preserve of the wealthy. Mass production of dolls' houses and dolls' house furniture began during the Victorian era, taking away their exclusivity and making them more widely accessible.

Peeking into dolls' houses now gives us a glimpse into the past: they speak to us across the centuries, telling us how people lived, revealing the architecture, furnishings, fashions, customs and social attitudes of their day, and showcasing the incredible craftsmanship of the people who created them. But if we want to experience the past, why focus on miniatures? There are plenty of real houses we can wander around to soak up the style and atmosphere of a particular era, so why explore the past through the prism of miniature houses?

A.C. Benson, co-editor of *The Books of the Queen's Dolls' House* (Methuen & Co Ltd, 1924), may have had the answer: 'There is great beauty in *smallness*. One gets all the charm of design and colour and effect, because you can see so much more in combination and juxtaposition.' Flora Gill Jacobs, who quoted Benson in *A History of Dolls' Houses* (Bell & Hyman, 1965), added: 'The ability to reflect, in a relatively limited amount of space, four centuries of architecture, household furnishings, and innumerable customs is practical as well as appealing.'

Dolls' houses are more than just small houses with collections of dolls and miniature objects. They are multi-dimensional works of art with stories to tell. As with any works of art, we can simply gaze in awe at their exquisiteness and admire the craftsmanship that brought them to life, or we can delve a little deeper to see what they have to say to us.

In *Portillo's Hidden History of Britain* (Michael O'Mara, 2018), Michael Portillo explores a selection of buildings, focusing on 'their beauty, their purpose, the stories hidden in their walls'. We can do exactly the same with dolls' houses, all of them fascinating slices of social history whose worth as historical objects became increasingly recognised during the twentieth century. This resulted in the emergence of several dedicated childhood museums and dolls' house collections, often putting long-neglected dolls' houses on public display for the first time.

Many dolls' houses, sadly, continue to languish in storage, which is entirely understandable: space in museums is limited and renovation is costly. It is a shame, though, to have these exquisite time capsules hidden from view, and I hope that some of those currently in storage might yet see the light of day. Happily, there are many fascinating and historically important dolls' houses on display, and one of the delights of writing this book has been visiting dolls' houses up and down the country and sometimes discovering them in unexpected places.

Between them, these dolls' houses capture, in miniature, a snapshot of more than 300 years of British domestic life.

Chapter 1

Early Baby and Cabinet Houses

'When the doors of a miniature house are opened, revealing comfortably furnished bedrooms, an elegant drawing room, or a kitchen equipped with every utensil imaginable, the magic is complete.'

Faith Eaton, *The Ultimate Dolls' House Book*
(Dorling Kindersley, 1994)

The fascination with all things miniature stretches back into antiquity. Archaeologists have unearthed tiny replicas of household items dating back to the ancient Egyptian, Greek and Roman civilisations, their purpose unclear but possibly intended as toys, ornaments or devotional objects. Excavations during the post-war redevelopment of the City of London yielded miniature Roman pottery and bronze miniatures from around the fourteenth century, but the most significant haul of tiny treasures in recent times was the collection of metal toys gathered from the Thames foreshore by mudlarker Tony Pilson.

Now at the Museum of London, the collection includes toy plates, bowls, jugs and ewers fashioned from lead alloy and dating from the thirteenth and fourteenth centuries. It is reasonable to assume that these miniatures were made for dolls' houses. The collection – which also features toy knights and cannons – shed new light on medieval childhood and led to the 2004 publication of *Toys, Trinkets and Trifles: Base Metal Miniatures from London 1200 to 1800* by Hazel Forsyth and Geoff Egan.

German Baby Houses

For the first known dolls' house, we have to travel forwards from the Middle Ages to sixteenth century Bavaria where Duke Albert V (1528–79), apparently not content with his real-life ducal palace, decided he needed a miniature version too. In 1557 he commissioned a team of craftsmen to create and furnish what became known as the Munich Baby House, which was completed the following year. It is possible that it was originally intended for the duke's young daughters, Maria Anna and Maximiliana Maria, then aged 6 and 5, but it finished up in his already extensive collection of art, antiques and curios. It is unlikely the little girls ever played with it, but they may have been permitted to look and admire.

It's just as well the duke wasn't around in 1674, because he would have seen his precious miniature dream go up in smoke during a fire at the ducal palace. We would probably never have known about the baby house had it not been for one of the duke's councillors, Johann Baptist Fickler, who in 1598 had the presence of mind to draw up a detailed inventory of the miniature palace and its contents. This inventory has survived, and reveals the extent of the opulence and splendour of the palace, thus giving an insight into how the German aristocracy lived in the sixteenth century.

Highlights of the four-storey palace were its lavishly decorated ballroom, complete with musical instruments, silver serving dishes and rich Oriental carpet, the luxurious bedrooms with their hanging tapestries and exquisite bed linen, and the well-appointed bathroom and cosy nurseries. No expense was spared on the soft furnishings, many of which were made from silks and satins, both luxury materials that at the time were affordable only for the upper classes.

The duke's miniature palace may have been relatively short-lived, but the trend for grand, ornate baby houses – so called because they were 'baby' versions of real houses – continued, and by the beginning of the seventeenth century owning a baby house had become fashionable among the German aristocracy and wealthy middle classes.

Early baby houses were usually fairly simple wooden cabinets, with just a hint of exterior architectural detail. The main focus was on the expensive treasures within that showed off the affluence and social standing of their owners and often reflected the contents of their own homes. For those a little lower down the social scale, baby houses were aspirational rather than being truly representational, intended to given an impression of wealth and status.

Contrary to their name, the baby houses were often impressively large. The earliest surviving baby house, the Nuremberg House (1611), stands 9ft high, features three storeys and reflects a style typical of the Nuremberg town houses of the time. The house sits on a heavy base concealing a cellar, with a formal garden and Great Hall on the ground floor, the kitchen – as was usual at the time – on the first floor alongside the drawing room, and a bedroom and dining room above.

The Great Hall is notable for a large tapestry-effect mural depicting a garden party, complete with jester and musicians providing entertainment. The overall scene is one of carefree abandonment by upper-class folk in the kind of large, ornamental garden associated with grand dwellings, and is somewhat at odds with the rather more austere furnishing in the hall itself.

The rooms above are more luxurious. The formal drawing room features finely carved wooden furniture (most of it post-dating the baby house) and decorative swags along the upper part of the walls, while china and pewter ornaments are a feature of the dining room.

The house is on display at the Germanisches Nationalmuseum in Nuremberg, which was the centre of the German toymaking industry for more than 300 years.

A slightly later model, also on display at the Germanisches Nationalmuseum, is the Stromer baby house (1639), which has fourteen incredibly detailed rooms giving an accurate insight into a wealthy family home in seventeenth-century Nuremberg. A delightful looking house, it has an impressive arched entrance flanked by columns, decorative balustrades along the front of the first and second floors, a grand central staircase, miniature portraits in most of the main rooms, wooden panelling, green ceramic stoves and attractively draped four-poster beds in the two bedrooms.

The museum also has two slightly later baby houses: the Kress and Bäumler houses, both of which date from the late seventeenth century and reflect the beginning of a trend towards more interesting architectural details.

The Kress baby house, originally owned by the Kress von Kressenstein family of Nuremberg, features eye-catching twin gables with simple carved scrolls, but its crowning glory is still very much the interior; like Stromer, it has ornate balustrading across the two upper floors and carved wooden panelling, with the addition of theatrical proscenium arches framing the main rooms. A family of dolls was added in the eighteenth century.

The Bäumler baby house has some attractive decorative carving around its base, while the roof features two symmetrically placed chimney stacks and two small gables flanking a central gable. Of particular note are the spiked metal stars on the roof, once a feature of Nuremberg homes but banned during the eighteenth century due to their inability to withstand strong winds.

One of the most extravagant creations of the early eighteenth century was Mon Plaisir, a miniature representation of the town of Arnstadt at the turn of the century, from its humblest dwellings to its stately homes and royal court. Commissioned by Princess Augusta Dorothea von Schwarzburg-Arnstadt, it consists of around eighty room settings populated by 400 dolls and is now on display in the Schlossmuseum in Arnstadt.

An educational role

Baby houses weren't just things to be admired – they had an educational role, too. For young ladies, many of them unable to read and write, they were the perfect way to illustrate the layout and efficient running of a typical family home.

An early example of a dolls' house built specifically for didactic purposes is one commissioned in 1631 by Nuremberg resident Anna Köferlin, who took it upon herself to instruct women, young girls and servants in the intricacies of domestic skills and efficient household management, charging them a small fee for the benefit of her wisdom. In an accompanying broadsheet, she exhorted her students to,

> look you then at this Baby House ... learn well ahead how you shall live in days to come. See how all is arranged in kitchen, parlour and bedchamber, and yet is also well adorned. See what great number of chattels a well-arrayed house does need ... hundreds of pieces. Of bedding, of handsome presses, of pewter, copper and brass, fitted up in such a way that though so small, yet everything may well be put to general use.

Anna's baby house no longer exists, but we can get an impression of it from the surviving broadsheet. Standing nearly 8ft high, just over 4ft wide and a little more than 3ft deep, its size would have made it an ideal demonstration model. Its style was typical of the Nuremberg houses at the time, with bottle-glass windows, a gabled roof, and a grand, arched entrance.

The V&A Museum of Childhood at Bethnal Green has a Nuremberg house dating from 1673, and this was almost certainly intended primarily as both a toy and an educational tool. At just 3ft 6ins high, and with only four rooms, it is much smaller and simpler than the grander Nuremberg houses and reflects a far less glamorous lifestyle.

The arched doorway and small-paned windows closely resemble those of a typical Nuremberg house of the late seventeenth century, and many of its original contents and features have survived, including its metal stars and dovecotes on the roof.

The ground floor kitchen, typical of the period, is generously equipped with a charcoal cooking stove, numerous pots, pans and cooking utensils in pewter and brass, large wooden casks and barrels for storing vinegar and salt, a large central table, and wooden cupboards and shelves providing plenty of storage space. Adjacent is a second kitchen/dining room, a cosy space featuring an impressive display of pewter plates and tankards on wooden shelving around the walls. There is also a privy tucked into the corner.

Upstairs are two bedrooms, one of which doubles as a sitting room. In the bedroom is a large wooden painted cabinet filled with bed linen, a feature of many real Nuremberg homes, as well as an elaborate wooden baby walker. The second bedroom/sitting room includes a simple wooden highchair and an intricately carved spinning wheel.

The overall effect is of a house that is small and cluttered, but one that would be perfect for teaching the art of domesticity to young ladies and their servants.

Dutch Cabinet Houses

By the late seventeenth century wealthy merchants in Holland had discovered a passion for miniatures, and these became symbols of the country's burgeoning economy. The founding of the pioneering Dutch East India Company in 1602, coupled with liberation from Spain in 1648 following the Eighty Years' War, heralded the start of the Dutch Golden Age. Amsterdam became the centre of world trade, and local merchants became extremely rich through the trading of goods such as spices, silk, tea, coffee, rice, sugar and wine across Europe, Africa and Asia.

On their travels, these merchants would collect precious items to bring home for display. Exotic shells, portrait miniatures and various items in gold, silver, pewter and porcelain were popular, and these were displayed in a 'cabinets of curiosities' as a statement of the owner's wealth and success.

From these developed the idea of the cabinet house for the merchants' wives, who created miniature rooms displayed within decorative wooden cabinets. By the turn of the century, a miniature cabinet house was an essential item in many a wealthy Amsterdam merchant's house and often formed part of a young lady's marriage dowry.

The cabinet houses were quite distinct from the German baby houses in that they were not intended as replica houses, nor as educational tools. These were elaborate showcases, filled with hundreds of exquisite, rare and valuable objects, intended as conversation pieces with which to impress visitors. In what seems a somewhat narcissistic exercise, the cabinet houses were often based on the owner's home and featured miniature copies of their own possessions.

In *English Dolls' Houses of the Eighteenth and Nineteenth Centuries* (Bell & Hyman, 1955), Vivien Greene, wife of novelist Graham Greene and doyenne of dolls' house collecting, suggested that the cabinet houses were 'perhaps less a personal hobby than an illustrated inventory, a boast of industry, good judgement and taste'.

The cabinets themselves were impressive pieces of furniture, as much part of the display as the treasures concealed behind their decorative doors. Commissioned from the finest craftsmen, they were usually made from a robust wood such as oak veneered with walnut or tortoiseshell, often inlaid with ivory or pewter, and supported by ornately carved legs. A small but important feature was a key; this alone told visitors that the cabinet's contents were so precious they needed to be kept locked away.

Surviving cabinet houses give us a vivid insight into the lives of wealthy merchants' families in seventeenth-century Amsterdam. The rooms are like a series of theatrical scenes, everything carefully placed for maximum effect, a moment frozen in time.

One of the earliest and most splendid belonged to Petronella de la Court (1624–1707), wife of a wealthy Amsterdam brewer. This elegant, sophisticated cabinet dates from around 1670 and its lavishly furnished rooms are filled with more than 1,600 tiny treasures.

Visitors admiring this unashamed display of extravagance would have marvelled at the engravings, classic busts and other *objets d'art* in the art room and salon, among which are paintings by Dutch artists Gerard Hoet (1648–1733) and

Frederik de Moucheron (1633–86). The art room also has its own tiny cabinet of curiosities.

In the formal garden on the ground floor, the eye is drawn to a central gazebo in white trellis, fronted by statues and surrounded by an abundance of flowers. Next door is a lying-in room, a common feature of Dutch houses at the time, where new mothers could rest in comfort and receive guests. Designed to impress, the lying-in room was typically filled with exquisite linen and precious ornaments, and guests would be offered luxury drinks and foodstuffs to remind them of the wealth and status of their host.

Now on display at the Centraal Museum in Utrecht, Petronella de la Court's cabinet has been arranged in accordance with an inventory compiled in 1758 by Margareta van der Beek, whose father, Pieter, owned the house from 1754.

A slightly later house, now at the Rijksmuseum in Amsterdam, was one commissioned in 1676 by Petronella Dunois (1650–95), the daughter of a court official in The Hague. The house formed part of her dowry when she married Pieter van Groenendijck the following year, and it remained in the family for over 250 years. The lying-in room is particularly luxurious with its chintz walls and matching bed linen, and the house is well populated with dolls dressed in fashions of the period.

Also at the Rijksmuseum is the cabinet house that belonged to Petronella Oortman (1656–1716), who married silk merchant Johannes Brandt in 1686. The house was commissioned in the same year and completed in 1690. The most remarkable room is the kitchen, which is clearly intended more as a showpiece than as a place to prepare food, and includes a decorative wooden cabinet displaying a collection of fine china. Other interesting features include the cabinet of curiosities displaying a collection of exotic shells, and various pieces of artwork in the entrance hall, lying-in room and tapestry room attributed to Johannes Voorhout (1647–1717) and Willem Frederiksz van Royen (1645–1723).

Amsterdam artist Jacob Appel (1680–1751) produced a painting of Petronella Oortman's cabinet house in 1710, using oil on canvas and parchment, and this is now on display in the Rijksmuseum. From this we can see that the house originally had protective yellow curtains and several dolls that sadly have not survived.

The cabinet house craze continued well into the eighteenth century, and the Kunstmuseum in The Hague contains a particularly splendid walnut cabinet house made by Dutch craftsman Jan Meijer in 1743. It was commissioned by Sara Ploos van Amstel-Rothé (1699–1751), who – somewhat controversially – combined the furnishings of three earlier cabinet houses to form one magnificent showpiece, which she filled with beautifully carved wooden furniture, miniature paintings, richly coloured rugs, fine ornaments and kitchenware in brass, silver, glass and china, and embroidered furnishings made by Sara herself.

The original cabinet houses, bought as an auction lot for 1,000 guilders in April 1743, were sadly destroyed, but Sara kept meticulous records of the changes she made and the names of the craftsmen involved.

The cabinet house style remains unique to Holland but was clearly an influence on the first English dolls' houses, which began to appear in the late seventeenth century and set a whole new trend in the miniature world.

Chapter 2

Ann Sharp's Baby House

'... this gentlewoman ... has left to posterity
playthings breathing an atmosphere of tender, old-
world romance ...'

> Mrs Willoughby Hodgson, *The Quest
> of the Antique* (Herbert Jenkins, 1924)

Ann Sharp, daughter of the Archbishop of York, was around
5 or 6 years old when her godmother, the future Queen
Anne, gave her the gift of a baby house. Thought to date
originally from between 1695 and 1700, this rare survival
from the closing years of the Stuart era gives an insight into
a typical upper-class town house of the late seventeenth and
early eighteenth centuries.

Ann Sharp's house has never been on public display, but
its history and contents have been well documented, notably
by early twentieth century antiques writer Mrs Willoughby
Hodgson and dolls' house specialist Vivien Greene. Mrs
Hodgson devoted a chapter to Ann Sharp's house in her
book *The Quest of the Antique* (Herbert Jenkins, 1924), and
this was also serialised in two parts in collectors' magazine
The Connoisseur.

Ann was born in 1691 to John Sharp, then the newly appointed Archbishop of York, and Elizabeth Palmer of Winthorpe, Lincs. She was one of fourteen children, of whom only four survived to adulthood. Her father's appointment to one of the most senior positions within the Church of England followed his swift rise from ordination as a deacon and priest in 1667 to becoming archdeacon of Berkshire (1673), Dean of Norwich (1681–89) and Dean of Canterbury (1689–91).

Growing up at Bishopthorpe, the official residence of the Archbishop of York, Ann would have been familiar with the upper echelons of society, from other senior church figures to aristocracy and royalty. This is reflected in the layout and contents of the baby house, particularly in the collection of wooden and wax dolls representing the family and their servants and labelled with names such as 'My Lord Rochett', 'Roger, ye butler', 'Fanny Long, the chambermaid' and 'Sarah Gill, ye child's maid'.

As Mrs Willoughby Hodgson puts it in *The Connoisseur*: 'From the arrangements which we find in this miniature home, we may gather interesting and enlightening facts about the manners and customs which obtained in a well-ordered household in the earliest days of the eighteenth century.'

This early baby house closely resembles the Dutch cabinet house in style, just one of many examples of the Dutch influence in England at the time following the coronation of William and Mary in 1689. It lacks the opulence of the Dutch cabinets, though; Vivien Greene described it as 'a plain glazed wooden' cabinet with an interior that, 'although fascinating to a degree, is neither luxurious nor full of fine art' (*The Vivien Greene Dolls' House Collection*, Cassell, 1995).

The lack of sophistication can be explained by the fact that – unusually for the time – this appears to have been intended as a child's toy rather than a showcase for an adult's expensive miniatures. As such, it gives us a window on a child's world in the late seventeenth century.

According to Mrs Willoughby Hodgson, 'one of the most interesting features of her dolls' house …' is that it has been 'preserved just as the little girl left it …' (*The Connoisseur*, 1917).

The cupboard is simple but elegant in pale green, with shaped cornice and legs. It stands 5ft 10in high and has four storeys consisting of nine rooms and an attic. As a child, Ann made many of the furnishings herself, including a wooden toy theatre (with a play in progress) and a cardboard dolls' house with cardboard furnishings. She continued to fill the baby house with miniatures until her death in 1771, resulting in an intriguing mix of expensive, finely crafted items and crudely made child's furnishings that together span a period of around eighty years.

On the top floor is Lady Rochett's chamber, a vision of lace-trimmed brocade and silk in pink and blue covering the bed and the elegant, ornamental dressing table. Cream lambs-wool blankets with an embroidered flower in one corner of each complete the luxurious look of the bed. Among the generous display of ornaments are some blue and white Chinese miniatures, which Hodgson tells us were 'at the time in great request, following, no doubt, the fashion introduced from Holland by Queen Mary'. Walnut stools and tables decorated with imitation marquetry – another Dutch fashion – complete the scene.

Next door is Lady Rochett's dressing room, again elaborately decorated with a carved chandelier holding eighteen candles, alabaster tea table and tea set, silver teapot and coffee pot, walnut chairs and several ornamental tables. There is also a parrot in a cage and, rather strangely, a monkey wearing a shovel-shaped hat – both fashionable accessories in a well-to-do eighteenth-century household.

The most eye-catching item in this room, though, on the back wall, is the framed wax relief portrait of Mother Shipton, a legendary Yorkshire witch from the fifteenth century whose prophecies are said to have included the Great Fire of London. The inclusion of Mother Shipton in this baby house suggests that people in the Stuart era still believed in her uncanny powers more than a hundred years after her death in 1561.

A lying-in room/nursery features another magnificent bed, this time draped with embroidered green silk edged with silver lace, with a walnut cradle close by occupied by a tiny wax baby clad in swaddling clothes and a lace-edged cap. 'Sarah Gill, ye child's maid' keeps a watchful eye on her tiny charge. The tiny cardboard dolls' house, with its cardboard furniture, features tiny prints on the walls that Mrs Hodgson tells us 'are believed to represent Bishopthorpe'.

Beneath the lying-in room is the kitchen, where a pig is being roasted over a spit and a plum pudding is boiling in a copper pot – both popular delicacies of the period. Evidently guests are expected for dinner. The well-equipped kitchen includes a brass plate rack filled with pewter plates, a wooden dresser laden with utensils, copper bed-warming pans and much more.

Adjacent is the hall, which also doubled as the dining room. Preparations are underway for the guests, with an array of cold meats set out on the main dining table and other meats, including fowl and mutton, on a side table. The main table also has Charles II silver candlesticks. 'Roger, ye butler' is in attendance, dressed in a blue linen tunic and breeches, while a lady at the foot of the stairs, dressed in a red-striped silk dress edged with lace, is traditionally thought to be Lady Rochett.

Her husband is in the drawing room with the guests, including 'Lady Jemima Johnson', 'Mrs Lemon' and an unnamed lady, all dressed in the fashions of the day. Mrs Hodgson suggests that Ann Sharp probably modelled these ladies on real visitors to the family home. The drawing room is notable for its pink wallpaper with hand-painted gold embellishment, some more of the fashionable blue-and-white Chinese porcelain, and ivory poker, shovel and tongs on the hearth.

Ann's miniature portrait of Queen Anne, painted on the back of a playing card (the nine of diamonds) and placed in a dark oval frame, takes pride of place on the chimney breast – suggesting that Ann had a genuine affection for her royal godmother.

On the ground floor are the servants' quarters. 'Mrs Hannah, ye housekeeper' is in her bedroom, which is furnished with a walnut-framed mirror, walnut chair and a mahogany chest of drawers, on which stands a Staffordshire bottle and ewer. The four-poster bed, draped in white linen, looks cosy but is noticeably less grand than those on the top floor. A footman is in a rather more sparsely furnished room next door, and in the servants' hall beyond, another pig is being roasted on a spit. The room also contains a pair of rocking horses and some tiny figures, possibly belonging to the toy theatre in the nursery.

At the very top of the house is an attic, spanning the width of the house and used for storing additional items of furniture.

In addition to the baby house, Anne also at some point gave her goddaughter an illustrated, calf-bound prayer book.

In 1712 Ann married her father's chaplain, Heneage Dering, later Dean of Ripon. The marriage ceremony, unsurprisingly, was performed by Sharp, and the couple spent their honeymoon in Bloomsbury. Dering was nearly thirty years Ann's senior, and in the memoirs he began writing much later in life he recalled travelling with John Sharp, his wife and baby daughter, 'afterwards my wife'. Dering died in 1750, aged 86.

Ann and Heneage had a son, John, who later became Rector of Hilgay in Norfolk, and a daughter, Elizabeth, who married Charles Elsley, from the North Yorkshire village of Patrick Brompton, in 1739.

Elizabeth inherited the dolls' house after Ann's death in 1771 and it continued to be passed down through the generations, eventually to be inherited by the Bulwar-Long family of Heydon Hall, Norfolk. Vivien Greene recalled visiting the family to see Ann Sharp's house and reported that Mrs Bulwer 'was then herself 101 and lively as a flea' (*The Vivien Greene Dolls' House Collection*, Cassell, 1995). The house remains in private ownership, and stands alone as a unique and charming relic, in miniature, of an English upper-class home on the cusp of the Stuart and Hanoverian eras.

Chapter 3

Baby Houses in Georgian and Regency England

'Time stands still and a period is preserved as it never can be in a full-sized house. All sorts of things, however ephemeral, are left in a dolls' house that would never remain in a human's.'

Flora Gill Jacobs, *A History of Dolls' Houses*
(Bell & Hyman, 1965)

Magnificent cabinets with lavish interiors were all very well, but by the early eighteenth century people were starting to want realistic-looking houses in which to display their miniature treasures. Baby houses became fashionable among the English upper classes, and it wasn't long before they were abandoning the Dutch-style cabinet houses in favour of miniatures that were much more like replicas of real houses.

They were inspired, no doubt, by the grand, palatial mansions that became a feature of the English landscape during the eighteenth century. This was the heyday of the English country house – Woburn Abbey, Holkham Hall in Norfolk and Harewood House in Yorkshire being notable examples – and baby houses became miniature imitations of the real thing, lavishly designed and furnished to reflect the architecture and domestic life of the period.

The coronation of George I in 1714 came at a time of unprecedented national wealth. Under William and Mary, and later Anne, Britain had expanded rapidly to become one of Europe's most powerful trading nations, resulting in increased wealth and improved living standards across much of the population.

This new-found wealth was expressed in the imposing mansions that increasingly studded Britain's countryside as the century progressed, each a statement of the owner's status and power. Typically, a country house would be perched above acres of landscaped gardens and parkland, its lofty position a symbol of the owner's social superiority, and the interior was a repository for collections of paintings and other valuable objects.

Baby houses became important showpieces in these grand new homes, usually displayed in a prominent room where visitors would be sure to see them. Like the country house itself, the baby house was a statement of wealth, privilege and good taste.

Early Eighteenth Century Baby Houses

At the beginning of the eighteenth century, dolls' houses were still fairly simple and not unlike the Dutch cabinet houses. An example is the Heslington Baby House, currently on display at the York Castle Museum. It is similar in design to Ann Sharp's house, with nine rooms, three on each level, topped by a shaped cornice, but in white rather than green and with no attic. Like Ann's, though, this appears to have been intended as a toy rather than an adult showpiece.

The baby house was built for the Yarburgh family of Heslington Hall, York (now part of the University of York campus), in around 1700–20, probably by an estate carpenter. Although sometimes thought to have been the work of prominent architect Sir John Vanbrugh (1664–1726), this seems unlikely, despite there being a family connection: Vanbrugh married Henrietta Maria Yarburgh in 1719, when she was 26 and he 55. Despite the twenty-six-year age gap, their brief union – Vanbrugh died just seven years later – is believed to have been a happy one.

Much of the original content of the house has survived, including the dolls, furniture and kitchen fittings on the ground floor. Other objects were added by subsequent generations up to the 1930s.

An interesting feature is that the height of each level is noticeably smaller than the one below it. Within a few years, room height had become an indicator of importance: those of the greatest heights would be the ones where the family received visitors, while those of the lowest height would be the servants' quarters. Here, though, the smallest rooms at the top of the house are clearly family rooms as they are too well furnished for servants.

The Palladian Revival

By the 1730s, baby houses were beginning to look less like cabinets and more like miniature houses, and they reflected the Palladian-style architecture of the period.

The popularity of the Grand Tour – that educational 'rite of passage' around Europe undertaken by young men of the upper classes – inspired a renewed interest in classical antiquity during the late seventeenth and early eighteenth centuries. Architects looked once more to the work of Italian Renaissance architect Andrea Palladio (1508–1580), who had sought to emulate the grandeur of ancient Rome. Palladio's work was based on the belief that perfect proportions and symmetry were more aesthetically pleasing to the eye than elaborate ornamentation, and he used mathematics to achieve the desired effect.

The result was a reinterpretation of the classic Roman temple with a central portico, a pediment and decorative balustrade around the roof, flanked by wings of similar proportions. Some of the grander Palladian mansions were embellished with triumphal steps and cupolas.

The Palladian revivalists drew inspiration from Palladio's *I Quattro libri dell'architettura* (*The Four Books of Architecture*), which was published in four volumes in Venice in 1570. The first complete English translation was published in London between 1715 and 1720.

Inigo Jones (1573-1652) spearheaded the first Palladian revival in England in the early seventeenth century, and his notable works include the Queen's House at Greenwich, St Paul's Church at Covent Garden, and Banqueting House, Whitehall. During the early eighteenth century, Lord Burlington (1694–1753) was at the forefront of a second Palladian revival after studying Palladio's work during three Grand Tours, and gradually this elegant, restrained style took over from the more flamboyant English Baroque style epitomised by Sir Christopher Wren (1632–1723), Sir John Vanbrugh and Nicholas Hawksmoor (1661–1736).

It wasn't long before baby houses were being built by estate carpenters in the Palladian style. These miniatures were designed to impress, but they were also intended to instruct young ladies in the organisation and management of a country house. Two of the earliest and most historically significant baby houses to have survived from the early eighteenth century are those at Uppark in West Sussex and Nostell Priory in Yorkshire, both now in the care of the National Trust.

The Uppark Baby House

In 1746, a young lady by the name of Sarah Lethieullier, the daughter of a wealthy banker of French Huguenot descent, married Northumberland coal and wine merchant Sir Matthew Fetherstonhaugh. A year later, when the couple moved to Uppark in West Sussex, 25-year-old Sarah brought with her a Palladian-style dolls' house, believed to date from around 1735–40. The fact that the house has survived in such good condition suggests it was a showpiece rather than a toy, in keeping with the times, and it gives an accurate glimpse into Georgian domestic life above and below stairs.

The 1/12 scale dolls' house features nine rooms, a central pediment bearing the Lethieullier coat of arms, and a balustraded parapet topped with classical figures. The house sits on a five-arched pedestal, which may or may not be original, but it does match the colour and brick-effect of the house. The room heights are the opposite of those in the Heslington baby house: the smallest rooms are on the ground floor and include the kitchen, servants' dining room and housekeeper's room, while the largest rooms are on the middle floor and include the drawing room, dining room and principal bedroom. There are three more bedrooms on the top floor, with the grandest in the centre.

The contents are mostly original and include collectable items such as Japanese and Chinese porcelain, hallmarked silverware and English glassware – the kind of luxury miniatures previously displayed in the Dutch cabinet houses. The family rooms are lavishly filled with finely carved furniture in mahogany and ivory, imported silks and Flemish-style oil paintings. The 'below stairs' rooms are more plainly furnished, and the distinction between the two levels is emphasised with fashionably dressed wax dolls in the upstairs rooms and wooden, plainly dressed dolls representing the servants.

Some of the contents may have been added later, and there is evidence that the house has been repainted a couple of times.

By 1930, Uppark had passed to Sir Herbert and Lady Margaret Meade-Fetherstonhaugh, and the latter set about restoring the curtains in both the dolls' house and the main house using a detergent made from the herb *saponaria officinalis*. Vivien Greene, visiting Uppark to see the 'grand baby house', recalls seeing Lady Margaret washing the curtains 'using her special saponaria recipe' (*English Dolls' Houses of the Eighteenth and Nineteenth Centuries*, Bell & Hyman, 1955). She also notes that Lady Margaret 'had found the little statues that go on top of the baby house somewhere in the stables' – suggesting that the house may have been put in storage at some point before Lady Margaret rescued it and restored it to its former glory.

H.G. Wells and the Uppark baby house

Novelist Herbert George Wells – known to his family as Bertie – was 13 when his mother, Sarah Wells (née Neal), was appointed housekeeper at Uppark in 1880. School holidays were spent exploring the attic, devouring the books in the library and occasionally being allowed to play with the dolls' house under strict supervision. Wells drew on his childhood days at Uppark when writing his 1909 novel *Tono-Bungay*, in which Uppark is thinly disguised as Bladesover, his mother as the housekeeper Mrs Ponderevo, and himself as her son, George.

The young George Ponderevo is overawed by the 'great splendid' toys in the nursery, which are 'gigantic to all my previous experience of toys', and revels in the fact that 'we even went to the great dolls' house on the nursery landing to play discreetly … I played under imperious direction with that toy of glory'. Back at school, George writes 'a great story out of the doll's house' which, with his friend Ewart, 'speedily grew to an island doll's city all our own'.

Nostell Baby House

Similar in style to the Uppark baby house, and again dating from around 1735–40, is the baby house at Nostell Priory, a magnificent mansion near Wakefield in Yorkshire. This spectacular miniature was created around the same time as Nostell itself, and is a rare example of a baby house still existing in the property for which it was built. It was commissioned by Sir Rowland Winn, the 4th baronet, for his wife, Lady Susanna Henshaw, who was responsible for much of the interior decoration. Many of its features mirror those of the main house, possibly reflecting Lady Susanna's aspirations for her new home.

Tragically, Lady Susanna didn't get to enjoy the baby house for long as she died in childbirth in 1741, aged 32, before the main mansion was completed.

As well as sharing some features with Nostell, the baby house also closely resembles the Winns' former home of Thornton Hall, a late seventeenth-century country house in the Lincolnshire village of Thornton Curtis. The most noticeable similarities are the modillion cornice between the two upper storeys and the arched mouldings over the ground floor windows and front door.

Like Uppark, the Nostell baby house consists of nine rooms on three levels, with a similar balustraded parapet and statues, and is notable for the elegance and precision of its contents. The finely crafted furniture is attributed to Thomas Chippendale (1718–1779), who also provided much of the furniture for the real Nostell, and the tiny paintings were commissioned from leading artists of the day.

An unusual feature is the eye-catching staircase in the hallway, which begins vertically then turns horizontally as it sweeps majestically to the first floor. Stand-out items include the ivory inlaid cabinet in the drawing room, the hallmarked silver *objects d'art*, a walnut card table with cabriole legs, a longcase clock and the finely carved door pediments throughout.

The grand, elaborate fireplaces were copied from *A Book of Architecture* by James Gibbs (1682–1754), one of the leading architects of the eighteenth century whose masterpieces include the Radcliffe Camera in Oxford and the Church of St Martin-in-the-Fields at Trafalgar Square.

The kitchen is well stocked, as would have been expected in a country house of this era, with an abundance of copperware and earthenware pots and pans, and a rare floor-standing wooden plate rack to heat the dishes in front of the fire.

The dolls are in authentic period dress, and once again the distinction is made between upstairs and downstairs with wax dolls for the family and wooden dolls for the servants.

The Nostell baby house has recently been put back on display after a £100,000 conservation project, and is now in a new permanent exhibition space with state-of-the-art lighting to highlight the tiniest details of this extraordinary miniature.

Late Georgian Splendour

Two particularly fine late Georgian baby houses, both dating from around 1760 and built in the style of Palladian town houses, are the Tate baby house at the V&A Museum of Childhood and the Blackett baby house at the Museum of London.

Both feature an exterior balustraded double staircase, arranged symmetrically, as seen in early Neo-Palladian houses such as the Queen's House in Greenwich (Inigo Jones, 1616), Kedleston Hall in Derbyshire (James Paine, Matthew Brettingham and Robert Adam, 1759) and Chiswick House in London (Lord Burlington, 1727–29).

The staircase leads to the first floor, thereby drawing the eye upwards to the main part of the house (the *piano nobile*) and bypassing the servants' quarters on the ground floor. The Tate staircase is the grander of the two, with its three curved flights on each side, while the Blackett staircase resembles a triangle with its two single flights sweeping directly upwards.

The layout of the two baby houses is also similar, with the four main family rooms, all lavishly furnished, flanking a central hallway and landing. Both are topped with a balustrade, but the Tate house also has two chimneys and a skylight while the Blackett house has an additional upper gallery used for storing furniture.

The Blackett Baby House

The Blackett house is believed to have been a gift from Sir Edward Blackett, 4th Baronet, to his wife, Lady Anne Blackett, to celebrate the birth of their son, William, in 1759. The Blackett family owed their wealth to the Northumberland lead mines, and Sir Edward was a prominent public figure, serving as High Sheriff of Northumberland from 1757–58 and as MP for Northumberland from 1768–1774. Lady Anne (née Douglas) was the heiress to Matfen Hall in Northumberland.

The sumptuous furnishings and layout of the baby house are likely to be an accurate reflection of those in the Blackett family home, giving an idea of the typical lifestyle of a wealthy family in the late eighteenth century. The plush wallpaper, richly patterned carpets, framed paintings, elegant wooden furniture, soft furnishings, silver dining ware and fine ornaments in porcelain and glass all bear witness to their influence and social standing. Below stairs, as might be expected, is much more rudimentary, but the kitchen is well equipped. The lady of the house wears the latest fashions, while the servants in the kitchen and outside the ground floor door are dressed in simple, serviceable clothing.

The positioning of the Blackett baby house in the Museum of London's Expanding City gallery is a poignant one. Close by are the Wellclose Square debtors' cell (1750) and the door of Newgate Prison (c.1780), both of which were used to incarcerate the poor unfortunates who fell into debt. This juxtaposition of affluence and destitution emphasises the vast divide between the wealthy and the poverty-stricken in the eighteenth century.

The Tate Baby House

Making a similar statement of wealth and privilege is the Tate baby house, thought to have belonged to a Cambridge family and then passed down through several generations. This magnificent house was exhibited at the V&A Museum of Childhood in 1923, and became a permanent part of the collection after its last owner, Mrs Flora Tate, died in 1929. Unlike the Blackett house, it sits on a stand that was added in the early twentieth century, possibly by Flora Tate.

The attractive exterior features simulated brickwork in contrasting colours, with the *piano nobile* in light brown and the ground floor and quoining at the sides in cream. The balustrades, pediments and window frames are also in cream. The interior has been altered and added to over the years, including some of the wallpaper and ornaments, but the original mantelpieces, cornicing, carved mouldings and silver Dutch-style candelabra have survived. The house was constructed in three separate parts so that it could easily be taken apart for transporting.

A Royal Baby House

One of the more unusual survivals from the late eighteenth century is a baby house believed to have belonged to the daughters of George III, currently on display at Kew Palace in London.

This simple miniature dates from around 1780 and is a rare example from this era of a baby house that seems to have been intended as a child's toy rather than as an adult showpiece. It was made by one of the Royal Yacht carpenters, who adapted an old cupboard into a fairly rudimentary baby house with just two large rooms, one up and one down, plus a narrow hallway and landing and a flight of wooden stairs. Its nautical connection is reflected in its resemblance to a bathing machine, the fashionable new seaside feature that evolved from the early eighteenth century as belief in the medicinal benefits of the sea began to take hold. George III himself gave royal approval to the bathing machine when taking a curative dip in the sea at Weymouth in 1789.

The contents and furnishings of the baby house have remained remarkably intact. Many were made by the young princesses, and are testament to their painting and needlework skills. Its greatest historical significance, though, is the fact that the interior closely resembles that of the first floor rooms at Kew Palace during the reign of George III, thus giving a fascinating glimpse into eighteenth-century royal domestic life and interior furnishing trends of the time.

Of note is the bright green verditer wallpaper, which gives a striking background to the two main rooms. Verditer, a natural blue or green pigment derived from copper carbonate, was widely used for wallpapers from the late eighteenth century onwards. Also of note are the fitted carpets, a fairly new phenomenon at the time; the elegant, wheel-back chairs in the style of furniture maker Charles Hepplewhite; and the exquisitely embroidered bed linen, working bed-pulls and samplers.

When the young princesses became too old for toys, they gave their baby house and its contents to the daughters of the Royal Yacht's Flag Captain, Sir George Grey, during a visit to Weymouth. By 1904 the house had passed to Sir George's granddaughter, Mary Bonham Carter, but later it mysteriously found its way to New York, where it finished up in the care of an art dealer after failing to sell at auction. In 2004, it was offered to Kew Palace, and finally the baby house returned home.

The baby house proved an important artefact for Kew Palace conservators when recreating the palace's eighteenth-century interior during a major restoration programme from

1996–2006. Some of the baby house contents were in poor condition and had to be restored by specialist conservators. The fragile surface of the wallpaper was gently cleaned with saliva, as modern cleaning agents would be too harsh. Many of the soft furnishings, particularly those on the first-floor four-poster bed, were also carefully cleaned and replaced in their original positions.

The restored palace reopened to the public in 2006 with the baby house on display in the King's Breakfast Room, among other articles relating to the childhood of George III and his family.

Regency Elegance

In 1811, the famous 'madness' of George III – now believed to have been caused by bipolar disorder or porphyria – catapulted his decadent, profligate and fun-loving son, the Prince of Wales, into the seat of power as Prince Regent. After his father's death in 1820, the prince reigned for a further ten years as George IV.

Charming, flamboyant and extravagant, the prince attracted admiration for his good taste in art and architecture and for his patronage of the arts, but he was also despised by many for his gambling, womanising, heavy drinking and lack of leadership during the Napoleonic Wars. His ambitious architectural revolution plunged him deeply into debt but resulted in spectacular buildings, elegant urban terraces and majestic crescents, making the Regency era synonymous with glamour, elegance, culture and refinement.

John Nash's magnificent Brighton Pavilion, commissioned in 1787 and completed in 1822, was the Prince Regent's lavish seaside retreat and the pinnacle of his extravagance. The Chinese-inspired interior by Frederick Crace (1779–1859), with its colourful and exotic charm, reflected the vogue for chinoiserie, a Western interpretation of Chinese decorative art that first appeared during the late seventeenth century and gained in popularity throughout the Georgian and Regency eras. Chinoiserie featured in many a country house during this period, and inevitably found its way into dolls' houses.

The Killer Cabinet House

A notable example of chinoiserie in miniature is the cabinet house commissioned by the Manchester-born Dr John Egerton Killer in 1830 for his daughter, Frances Leigh Killer, and based on a favourite display cabinet in the Killer household. It is a striking piece, made with lacquered wood and featuring a shaped top and decorative legs reminiscent of the Dutch cabinet houses. It has been painted black and features Chinese buildings and figures on each door, painted in gold, with gold-leaf patterning above and on the stand and legs.

The doors open to reveal more chinoiserie on the insides of the doors, this time flowers and birds painted in a deep red on black.

There are four rooms – drawing room and bedroom upstairs, and parlour and kitchen on the ground floor – each decorated and furnished by Mrs Killer and her daughters in styles that reflect the gradual change from the Regency through to the very early Victorian era. Mass production meant that wallpapers were newly available in the late Georgian and Regency eras, and the boldly patterned wallpapers here, continuing the birds and flowers theme of the chinoiserie, were probably offcuts from the Killers' own home.

The drawing room features a Regency sofa, ornate chandelier, simple fireplace with gold mirror above, a bold-patterned carpet and dolls dressed in the fashions of the day. The furniture was probably bought from London manufacturers, but the samplers either side of the fireplace and the red cloth covering the wooden coffee table were probably handmade. What is particularly noticeable is the relaxed, informal scene here, in contrast to the formality of the earlier Georgian era.

That same informality and simplicity can be seen in the bedroom, apart from the very grand four-poster bed with its beautiful linen and drapes and its golden crown-like structure on the top. The wallpaper is a striking design of birds and flowers, offset by another bold-patterned carpet.

The parlour is the most relaxed room of them all, with books and children's toys clearly visible, suggesting that this is where the family gathered to enjoy time together. Next door, the kitchen appears less cluttered than early Georgian kitchens, but it is well equipped with plain wooden furniture – including a dresser with crockery attractively displayed – and plenty of pots, pans and other cooking equipment.

The Killer Cabinet House is now part of the collection at the V&A Museum of Childhood, having been donated by a descendent of Mrs Killer in 1936.

Changing Attitudes to Childhood

A more relaxed attitude to childhood emerged during the late eighteenth century, with an increasing recognition of the importance of informal play. Portraits of children traditionally showed them in formal attire, with solemn faces and with toys featuring as status symbols rather than as playthings, but by the late Georgian era children were increasingly seen smiling and seemingly playing with the toys instead of merely posing with them.

This shift in attitude may have been at least partly influenced by novelist Maria Edgeworth (1768–1849), who in 1798 published her pioneering treatise *Practical Education*, in which she espoused the importance of early education through play. Curiosity and imagination were to be encouraged, she felt, and even children from well-to-do households should have simple toys rather than elaborate ones – or, better still, make their own:

> They should be provided with the means of amusing themselves, not with painted or gilt toys, but with pieces of wood of various shapes and sizes, which they may build up or pull down, and put in a variety of forms and positions; balls, pulleys, wheels and strong little carts proportioned to their age and to the things they want to carry in them, should be their playthings.

Children from poorer families, of course, had no option other than to fashion their own toys from whatever materials they could lay their hands on, but the idea that even wealthy children should make their own toys was revolutionary at a time when parents delighted in buying the most expensive and most fashionable toys for their offspring as a way of advertising their wealth and status.

There was an emphasis on outdoor play during the eighteenth century, but gradually nurseries began to fill with indoor, educational toys that developed children's learning, imagination and practical skills. For the first time, dolls' houses began to be seen as toys for children, rather than as showcases for adults, and young girls were encouraged to make things for their dolls' houses out of everyday household objects such as paper, cardboard, cotton reels, small boxes, scraps of material and anything else that could, with a little imagination, be made into a piece of furniture or a cover for a doll's bed.

Longleat Regency Dolls' House

A fine example of a dolls' house from the early Regency era, with objects made by its young owners, can be seen at Longleat Safari Park. Dating from 1811, this Palladian-style house was made by the estate carpenter for Lady Charlotte Thynne, the youngest of the three daughters of the 2nd Marquess of Bath. Although the house belonged to Charlotte, it would almost certainly have been played with and furnished by all three girls. The eldest, Lady Elizabeth (1795–1866), later became Countess Cawdor;

the middle daughter, Lady Louisa (1801–1859) became the Countess of Harewood; and Charlotte herself became the Duchess of Buccleuch and Queensbury, and was Mistress of Robes to Queen Victoria in 1841–46. She had eight children of her own, and it is likely that they also played with the house.

The original dolls, wallpaper and curtains have survived, but other period items have been added over the years, often not to scale. Most of the furniture was made by the Thynne girls, some of it from playing cards covered in fabric, and it is likely they also made the bed coverings and cushions as a way of practising their needlework skills.

Not all of the furniture was made by the Thynne girls, though. In one of the upstairs rooms is a set of delicate, intricately carved white furniture, possibly made from bone or ivory, and believed to have been the handiwork of prisoners during the Napoleonic war.

Other items, of uncertain origin, include a silver-plated cot, a fragile bureau with its own minute key and inside mirror, a four-poster bed bearing the date 1804, and a coal scuttle filled with real coal. An elegant, curved staircase winds its way through the heart of the house.

The library is an impressive sight with rows of authentic-looking books made from card. A star exhibit is the tiny copy of Bryce's English Dictionary, which measures 25mm × 13mm and has its own case and magnifying glass. In the drawing room is a fire screen with a picture that becomes 3D when lit from behind.

Nunnington Hall baby house

This simple, four-room baby house was made in 1810 but has furniture, wallpapers and carpets reflecting the late eighteenth century. Of note are the exquisitely carved surrounds of a set of four chairs in the parlour, which are unlike styles of the time, and the eighteenth-century dolls made in Grodenthal in the Austrian Tyrol. The baby house belonged to Margaret Fife (née Rutson), who inherited Nunnington Hall from her uncle Henry in 1920, and bequeathed it to the National Trust on her death in 1952.

Audley End

A slightly later example is the dolls' house at Audley End in Essex. The rather plain exterior of this three-storey house conceals a magnificent interior, which almost certainly reflects domestic life at Audley End in the early nineteenth century. The house was probably built around 1825 by an estate carpenter for the eight children of Richard Griffin, 3rd Baron Baybrooke (1783-1858), and is lavishly furnished with richly coloured curtains, fine bed linen and elegant wooden furniture. The children contributed to the interior, using offcuts of fabrics and papers from the main house.

One of the standout items in the dolls' house is a decorative chest made by furniture maker John Bubb and painted in the fashionable chinoiserie style, possibly by the Braybrooke children's grandmother. There is also a rare blue washstand with floral design made by Wolverhampton toymaker Evans and Cartwright, a rare Nuremberg chair with ornate back and needlework seat, and other fine pieces of furniture and porcelain.

The death of George IV in 1830 saw his younger brother, William, come to the throne for a brief seven-year reign as William IV. By then Princess Victoria, who was to be the last of the Hanoverian line, was waiting in the wings, heralding the start of another seismic shift in Britain's domestic, cultural and political landscape.

Chapter 4

Victorians and the Age of Enterprise

'I tried at first making dolls' houses and taking them about for sale ... It was no good ... I couldn't sell any, so at last I went to the firm I work for now and they gave me employment.'

London dolls' house maker, quoted in
The Girls' Realm Annual, 1901

The Victorian era was ushered in with all the new-found confidence and prosperity of the Georgian era, leading to a new age of unprecedented invention, enterprise and industry. Advances in technology transformed Britain's productivity, making it one of the world's leading industrial nations. This was the age of Brunel, of steam power and railways, of colonialism and the expansion of the British Empire. The hugely successful Great Exhibition of 1851, a personal triumph for Prince Albert, was an expression of Victorian self-confidence and sense of achievement, an extravagant showpiece for the world.

Nineteenth-century inventions, such as the telephone, electric light bulbs, carpet sweepers and other domestic luxuries, soon found their way into contemporary dolls' houses. At the beginning of the century these continued to be largely in the hands of the wealthy, and the estate carpenters were still kept busy crafting dolls' houses and furniture. By the mid-nineteenth century, though, all this was beginning to change. New technology meant that dolls' houses could be produced more quickly and efficiently. Commercial toymakers began to appear on the scene, making dolls' houses and other toys more accessible to the middle and working classes. By the end of the century, mass production was well established.

Wealth was more attainable than ever before, with the growth in industries increasing the earning potential for a greater section of the population. The disparity between rich and poor persisted, though, and dolls' houses of the era reflect the stark contrast between the elaborate, over-filled houses of the wealthy and the austerity of those belonging to the working classes.

Architecture moved on from the neo-classical styles of the Georgian and Regency eras to Gothic-style suburban villas, often semi-detached and characterised by decorative gables, patterned brickwork, bay windows, painted panel doors and balconies. Interiors typically had eye-catching wallpapers in strong colours and patterns, decorative fireplaces, picture rails, coving and skirting boards. The new middle classes were keen to display their new-found wealth and status, and many a Victorian parlour or drawing room boasted elaborate furniture and impressive collections of paintings and ornaments. Card tables and pianos also became popular.

Grand mansions continued to appear, notably Queen Victoria's magnificent Isle of Wight retreat, Osborne House, built between 1845 and 1851.

At the other end of the scale were the notorious back-to-back slum houses, where overcrowding and disease were rife. Charles Dickens exposed the yawning chasm between rich and poor in nineteenth century Britain in his articles and novels, and some of the great philanthropic ventures arose during this era, including the ragged school movement (1844), the Salvation Army (1865) and Dr Barnardo's (1867).

The Invention of Childhood

The new, relaxed attitude to childhood that had emerged by the early nineteenth century came of age during the Victorian era. Discipline was still strict, and in wealthy households children saw more of the servants and governesses than they did of their parents, but it was now considered acceptable for children to have fun and to enjoy their innocent, carefree days before entering adulthood.

This change in attitude came from Queen Victoria and her consort, Prince Albert, who were often pictured with their children in a relaxed, informal family group. Both Victoria and Albert were skilled artists themselves, and they enjoyed producing sketches and paintings that provided snapshots of their children at play. Together, they encouraged the idea of the perfect family, in which children were cared for, protected and permitted to enjoy themselves.

There was still a strong belief in the value of learning through play, and Victorian nurseries gradually filled up with a mixture of toys that were both fun and educational. Jigsaw puzzles and board games that taught children about geography, history and the Bible were popular, as were mechanical, optical and scientific toys. Rocking horses, which had first appeared during the seventeenth century, were a common sight in many a Victorian nursery, and a Noah's Ark, with its biblical connection, was considered essential.

Imaginative play was also strongly encouraged, and castles, forts, toy soldiers, steam trains and toy theatres were all popular. For children, the appeal of these toys was that they were miniatures of real, familiar things.

Included in this category, of course, is the dolls' house, which now finally shed its image as an adult 'cabinet of curiosities' and became a child's toy, filled with furniture and other domestic items in contemporary styles along with dolls made in bisque, porcelain, wax or wood. Styles ranged from simple houses with just two rooms, one up and one down, to the more elaborate houses owned by children from wealthy households.

There would also have been plenty of homemade items, as making furnishings for a dolls' house was considered a useful way for boys and girls to learn practical skills such as carpentry and needlework. Instructional books and magazines began to emerge, notably *Boy's Own Toy-Maker* (1858) and *Girl's Own Toy-Maker* (1859) by wood-engraver and illustrator Ebenezer Landells, who had co-founded *Punch* in 1841.

Early Nineteenth Century Dolls' Houses

Up until the mid-nineteenth century, dolls' house manufacture in Britain was still largely in the hands of estate carpenters and independent craftsmen. Many of the latter were cottage industries, with one or more members of the family producing miniature houses that were often far grander than their own humble abodes – an irony that didn't escape Charles Dickens when writing *The Cricket on the Hearth* (1845), the story of toymaker Caleb and his daughter Bertha, whose living room doubled as their workshop. Here they made dolls' houses 'for dolls of all stations in life', including 'suburban tenements for dolls of moderate means' and 'capital town residences for dolls of high estate'. Some were 'filled on the most expensive scale … from whole shelves of chairs and tables, sofas, bedsteads and upholstery'.

Blaise Castle House Museum

A good example of a dolls' house from the early Victorian era can be seen at Blaise Castle House Museum near Bristol. Among the vast range of toys on display here, spanning the period between the eighteenth and twenty-first centuries, is a dolls' house that dates from around 1800 but has furniture and fittings that reflect the 1840s. It was commissioned by Bristol lawyer George Webb Hall and his wife, Maria, for their ten children, and was modelled on Maria's family home at 36 Queen Square, Bristol. There is significant wear to the base and to the cornice and pediment fronting the pitched roof, suggesting that the house was a well-loved toy for the young Webb children.

There are six rooms – kitchen, hallway and dining room downstairs, and nursery, landing and games room upstairs – and a central wooden staircase leading to the attic. The interior is generally well preserved and depicts a typical early nineteenth century household going about its daily business, from the ladies of the house in their lavish gowns to the more plainly dressed kitchen staff 'below stairs'. Some of the individual items are very finely detailed, including some tiny chess pieces in the games room on the first floor.

All rooms except the kitchen feature patterned wallpaper and fitted carpets, both still fairly new at the time, and the nursery, games room and dining room have marble-effect fireplaces with mirrors in elaborate gold frames above. The kitchen, as expected, is much plainer and simpler, but it is well equipped.

Particularly notable is the collection of pictures throughout the house. In the games room there are paintings of Tintern Abbey and George Webb in elaborate gold frames that complement the gold frame around the mirror on the chimney breast. Black and white pictures on the walls of the dining room are of Betws-y-Coed in Snowdonia and White House, Shrewsbury. The real showpiece, though, is a large tapestry in the hallway bearing the initials 'GWMH', and the Webb and Hall family shields. The names of George Webb and Maria Hall are written in pencil on the back.

The house was donated to the museum in 2001 by Anna Brandon-Jones, a descendant of the Halls, after being in the family for 200 years.

Bucks County Museum

The collections at this Aylesbury-based museum include an example of a carpenter-made house dating from 1845, which originated in the Buckinghamshire village of Long Crendon and was made for two local girls, Elisabeth and Sarah Loader. A simple square house, it has just four rooms and no staircase, and the rooms are furnished plainly but comfortably in styles of the period.

Ilkley Toy Museum

Among the vast range of dolls' houses here is the Stafford house, which dates from around 1830 and is a terrace of two houses featuring original brickwork, fanlights and tinplate toilet with working flush.

Mass Production

By the mid-nineteenth century, in response to the more relaxed attitude to childhood – and very much in the enterprising spirit of the age – commercial manufacturers were emerging and gradually taking over from the traditional toymakers. Mail order companies began to spring up after the introduction of the postal service in the 1840s, and toy shops such as Hamley's, which opened on Regent Street in 1881, gradually became more commonplace, selling dolls' houses and all that was needed to furnish and decorate them. For those that could afford them, owning a dolls' house had never been easier.

German manufacturers

By the end of the eighteenth century, Germany had already blazed a trail in toy manufacture and promotion, exporting dolls, dolls' house furniture and other toys to Britain and the Continent from places such as Nuremberg, Thuringia and Gröden. Wooden and tin toys were popular from these regions, as well as finely crafted items in bone and ivory. In 1803, Georg Bestelmeier, a Nuremberg merchant dealing in toys, textiles and fine arts, was one of the first to produce a marketing catalogue, an idea that gradually caught on during the nineteenth century.

Despite increased competition from British toymakers from the mid-nineteenth century onwards, Germany continued to dominate the market right up to the outbreak of the First World War. Early manufacturers included Rock & Graner (c.1813–1905), which specialised in decorative tinplate furniture, and Schneegas, which produced good quality dolls' house furniture up to the 1940s. Initially specialising in the popular Biedermeier furniture, a simple but decorative style with mahogany, rosewood or birch veneer, they later produced more elaborate pieces in the famous Waltershausen style, notable for its rosewood veneer, bone or ivory inlays, colourful silk upholstery and gilt paper trims. Examples of Schneegas furniture can still be seen in Victorian dolls' houses, including Amy Miles's house (see page 57).

Manufacturers to emerge in Germany during the latter half of the nineteenth century include Moritz Gottschalk (1865–1939; 1947–1972) from Marienberg, noted for his use of colour lithograph to create distinctive dolls' houses with porticos or castle-like turrets; Christian Hacker (1870–1914) of Nuremberg, known for his decorative, elegant houses;

and C. Moritz Reichel (1883 to 1972), which produced dolls' houses, room boxes and shops.

Meanwhile, toymakers from other countries were getting in on the act, notably in America, where one of the earliest (and eventually most popular) companies was the R. Bliss Manufacturing Company (1832–1914). Founded by Rufus Bliss in Pawtucket, Rhode Island, the company began producing wooden dolls' houses and dolls' house furniture in 1889, and again these stand out for their use of lithographed paper, usually in bold colours, the houses ranging in style from fairly simple to elaborate.

Miniature kitchens

Miniature kitchens, particularly the Nuremberg kitchen, were popular in Germany from the early nineteenth century onwards, usually featuring a hearth and filled with copper and pewter pots and pans, crockery and a variety of cooking implements. Intended as a teaching aid, the Nuremberg kitchen tended to be very detailed, although this could vary from simple versions to very elaborate ones.

An example of a well-filled Nuremberg kitchen from c.1800 is in the V&A Museum of Childhood collection, given by Mary Greg (see Chapter 10) in 1923. Ilkley Toy Museum has two kitchens, both from Germany. One, dating from c.1900, features lithographed paper, a printed oilcloth frieze, blue enamel cookware and a range of tinplate cooking equipment and pans. The other, dating from c.1905–10, is attractively decorated with Delft-style tiling, with coordinating blue enamel cookware and cream porcelain jugs and storage jars.

Shops

Similarly, miniature shops became popular in the early nineteenth century, mostly in mainland Europe, and their popularity continued right through to the twentieth century. Again, they were probably intended for educational purposes. Butcher's shops, with their large hanging joints of meat, are the most commonly found, but millinery, haberdashery and confectionery shops were also produced.

A late nineteenth century butcher's shop, made by Christian Hacker, is on display at the Old House Museum in Bakewell, Derbyshire, and there are also examples of butcher's shops at Worthing Museum and Art Gallery, the Museum of Childhood in Edinburgh and the Museum of Childhood at Sudbury Hall.

Ilkley Toy Museum has a set of miniature shops that were once part of the Evelyn Way Kendall collection and date from the 1840–50s. Canadian nurse Mrs Kendall was an avid collector of miniatures, and her collection was displayed in the Kendall Doll Museum in New England, USA, until it was auctioned off by Sotheby's in 1999.

The collection includes a glass shop, toy shop, pet shop and meat market. The shops are filled with finely crafted, incredibly detailed miniatures, from the delicate glass and china decanters, vases, figurines and animals in the glass shop to the lead, tinplate and wooden toys in the toy shop.

Most of the shops are populated by an assortment of papier mâché and wooden Grodnertal dolls.

Wooden peg dolls from the Grodnertal valley, dating from the early nineteenth century, had huge appeal due to their jointed limbs, brightly painted faces and decorative combs in their hair. They came in a range of sizes, including some small enough for dolls' houses. As a child, Queen Victoria had Grodnertal dolls among her vast collection and made clothes for them in the latest fashions.

Rigg House, Tunbridge Wells

This magnificent, large-scale house was made in Berlin in around 1840 and is a stunning example of early nineteenth century German craftsmanship. The house stands 8ft high and 5ft wide and has been built in the Palladian style, but the luxury décor and furnishings reflect the typical home of a wealthy family in early Victorian England. Some of the carpets and furniture were purpose-made in Brussels, with several later additions and alterations made by the Rigg family, after whom the house is named.

The Rigg family acquired the house in 1936, although their connection to the house goes back further than that. It is not clear who owned the house originally, but at some point it passed to two sisters, the daughters of a London stockbroker. One of them, Mrs Searle, was a missionary in Buenos Aires who adopted the three young Rigg brothers when their parents died, and she and her sister brought them up.

When Mrs Searle died in July 1935, aged 87, she left the dolls' house to her housekeeper, Mrs Pegram, who gave it to the wife of Dr Rigg, the eldest of Mrs Searle's adopted sons.

Mrs Rigg had various repairs carried out by her chauffeur and made several alterations, including the addition of the chimneys and the balconies on the upstairs windows, the uprights of which were made from miniature skittles cut in half. The house was acquired by Tunbridge Wells Museum & Art Gallery in 1957.

The house has four large rooms, two up and two down, as well as a hallway, staircase and landing, and a small under-stairs toilet. Elaborately patterned wallpaper graces every room except the kitchen, and there are functioning pull-down blinds at the front windows and plush, richly coloured curtains at the side windows. The whole house is a picture of elegance, refinement and opulence, from the marble-surround fireplace, chaise longue, sumptuous floor-length curtains, gold-framed mirrors and paintings in the parlour to the lavishly furnished dining room with its porcelain tea set, elaborate candlesticks and floor-length red curtains.

In contrast, the kitchen is plain and functional, with white wooden cupboards, shelves and sink unit, a wooden Welsh dresser and pine-effect wooden table. Various pots and pans, plates and glasses adorn the shelves and walls. A cosy fireplace, with a white wooden surround to match the rest of the kitchen, gives the room a homely, relaxed look.

The hallway reveals the grand sweep of the staircase, and there is an elaborately carved wooden coat stand against the left-hand wall. Beyond this, a door has been left slightly ajar so that you can just see the under-stairs toilet with its wooden seat and surround, and a toilet roll holder added by Mrs Rigg.

At the time of writing, the dolls' house is not on display as the museum has been closed for refurbishment. It is expected to reopen in 2021.

Early British Manufacturers

The father-and-stepson partnership of John Evans and Sydney Cartwright became famous during the first half of the nineteenth century for the manufacture of tinplate dolls' house furniture and other goods. The Wolverhampton-based firm was established by Evans in 1802 at a factory known as Whistle Hall (now sadly demolished), with Cartwright running the company from the 1820s.

The furniture pieces were made from tinplate and then japanned (i.e. covered with layers of resin-based varnish) to give a wood-like appearance, and were produced in Regency and William IV styles. Furniture for all rooms of a dolls' house, as well as kitchen equipment and fireplaces, came out of Whistle Hall right up to the early 1880s, despite a slump from the 1840s as Americans started their own toy manufacture and stopped English imports.

In his short story *A Christmas Tree* (1845), Charles Dickens describes the decoration of a traditional Christmas tree, including 'various other articles of domestic furniture (wonderfully made, in tin, at Wolverhampton)', a clear reference to Evans and Cartwright.

Another manufacturer from the early nineteenth century is London furniture maker John Bubb, who operated from Bermondsey in around 1810–40, turning his hand to dolls' houses and dolls' house furniture that was either made or veneered with mahogany. His work is easily identifiable by the imprinted 'john bubb maker' underneath each piece.

One of the best-known companies to emerge during the latter half of the nineteenth century was the London-based Silber & Fleming, which operated from around 1856 to 1898 as a manufacturer, importer and wholesaler of 'fancy goods'.

Silber & Fleming is most commonly associated with the tall, narrow 'box back' houses that became popular in the late nineteenth century due to the fact that they were reasonably priced and therefore accessible to many. They were also robustly built, making them ideal toys for young children. It is hard to say how many of the houses attributed to Silber & Fleming were actually manufactured by them and how many were made by other, anonymous manufacturers. It is thought that many were imported from Germany, while others were manufactured in England.

The company was relatively short-lived, lasting from 1856 to 1898, but it helped pave the way for other British manufacturers. The Lines brothers began trading as G&J Lines Ltd in 1876, initially making their mark as rocking horse manufacturers but becoming famous for their very recognisable range of dolls' houses during the early decades of the twentieth century. Similarly, Hobbies of Dereham launched late in the nineteenth century and came into its own in the twentieth century as a major supplier of dolls' house plans and fittings, while the English Toy Company, founded in 1889, produced Dollie Daisy Dimple, who had her own villa as well as a large wardrobe of clothes in the very latest fashions.

Late Victorian Dolls' Houses

By the late Victorian period, large numbers of dolls' houses were being commercially made, but the preference for dolls' houses made by estate carpenters or independent toymakers persisted through to the end of the century. Some particularly splendid dolls' houses have survived from this period, many of them reflecting the comfortable domestic lives of wealthy families of the nineteenth century.

Stanbrig Eorls

A particularly lovely survival from the late Victorian era is Stanbrig Eorls (pronounced 'Earls'), an elegant, three-storey white house dating from 1897 and now in the care of the Museum of Childhood in Edinburgh. It was created for 4-year-old Lena Montgomery and modelled on her childhood home, an Elizabethan house in Hampshire that later became a school.

The house has been lavishly but comfortably furnished, and at some point a white tower was added to the eastern end of the house to accommodate Lena's growing collection of miniature objects. Over the years she filled it with more than 2,000 items, some of them antique. The house now has eighteen rooms, complete with electric lighting and running water. An article about the house in the Christmas

1961 issue of *Illustrated London News* reported that it had even had its own burst water pipe, causing damage to the wallpaper near the staircase, and in 1932 there was a small fire caused by a short circuit.

As a child, Lena enjoyed making up stories about the house and its occupants, with her favourite doll, Nellie Bligh, 'the mistress of the house', playing a central role. In her *History of the House and the Bligh Family*, Lena recalled the true story of how Nellie was a Christmas tree ornament at Dudley House in Park Lane before being presented to her Nan by the Prince of Wales, later Edward VII.

Her imagination then took over as she presented poor Nellie with three successive husbands in a rather absurd story:

> The first was a fair-haired little man who, after a few years, suddenly disappeared. She waited a long time ... but at last she gave up hope and found another husband ... soon afterwards her first husband reappeared, so she engaged him as her gardener, but he soon died of a broken heart.

The second husband rather gruesomely loses both legs in an accident but is somehow able to be employed as Nellie's chauffeur. A third husband, 'a tall, stately gentleman', evidently survives because he becomes 'grey from old age'.

The adult Lena produced meticulous, handwritten lists of objects in the house, now in the museum's archives.

During the Second World War she toured the country with Stanbrig Eorls, raising money for the war effort and producing a brochure that she sold for one shilling.

Lena presented Stanbrig Eorls to the museum shortly before her death in the 1960s.

Amy Miles's House

Dating from the 1890s, this dolls' house appears to have been commercially made. Despite Vivien Greene feeling that there was 'a kind of towering absurdity about this house' (*English Dolls' Houses of the Eighteenth and Nineteenth Centuries*, Bell & Hyman, 1955), and despite the rather odd-looking extension added to the right of the staircase, it is exquisite in its elegant and lavish furnishings. Its main interest, though, lies in the abundance of new gadgets and technology that show the huge transformation that had taken place in domestic life throughout the Victorian era.

The bathroom has a water heater, enamel bath and plumbing, all of which had been developed from the 1870s; the kitchen also features a plumbed-in sink and a free-standing stove. Another contemporary feature in the bathroom and hallway is the sanitary wallpaper, one of the first washable wallpapers, which appeared in the late nineteenth century. The tile pattern seen in Amy Miles's bathroom was a particularly popular one at the time.

The invention of the electric light bulb by Thomas Edison and Joseph Swann in the late 1870s meant that electric lighting gradually replaced gas lighting in Victorian homes, and Amy Miles's house is lit by electricity throughout.

In the scullery is a safety bicycle, invented in 1885, and the hallway features a telephone, which first began to appear in Victorian homes from the late 1870s.

Other interesting features of this house include the collection of paintings in most rooms of the house, the Schneegas furniture in the nursery and schoolroom and other furniture in the house that is probably of German or French origin. The nursery is a typically Victorian nursery, with a rocking horse, dolls' house, model ships, a doll's cradle and a frieze featuring a design by artist and children's book illustrator Cecil Aldin (1870–1935).

Amy Miles lent her dolls' house to the V&A in 1915 for its *Children's Room* exhibition, and it became a permanent part of the collection in 1921.

Other examples of late nineteenth century dolls' houses among the V&A collections include Mrs Bryant's Pleasure and the Drew House, both dating from 1860, the very grand Risley villa from 1889 and a box back terrace house from the 1890s.

Hammond House

There are a few mysteries surrounding the Hammond House. Who made it? How did it come to be lying abandoned in an attic? Where did the name Hammond come from?

This exceptionally splendid three-storey house stands 9ft wide, just over 3ft high, and a little more than 4ft deep, and is very striking in appearance with its red-brick paper background and contrasting white wood. Probably commercially made, it has thirty-nine rooms, connected by corridors running the length of the house, and is fully furnished and lit with electricity throughout. The house also once had a working lift and running water in the bathroom and scullery. There are around 1,500 pieces of original furniture, most of it French and German, and the seventy-seven china dolls reflect a typical wealthy family of the late Victorian era with a master, mistress, family and servants.

In 1971, the *Newcastle Evening Chronicle* (13 February) reported that the house was being restored after being rescued from an attic, where it had apparently been gathering dust for fifty years, and given anonymously to the National Trust for display at Wallington, Northumberland. Vivien Greene, by then an acknowledged expert on dolls' houses, told the paper: 'I think it is a fantastic and lucky find. It is the biggest house I have ever seen.'

The original owner is believed to have been Ruby Hammond, whose name appears on a tiny towel and in a miniature copy book, but no information has been discovered about her.

The Hammond House is part of Wallington's collection of eighteen dolls' houses.

Pollocks Toy Museum

This historic museum, in the centre of London, has a large collection of Victorian dolls' houses with original furnishings and wallpapers, which give an accurate glimpse into the lives, fashions and tastes in décor of well-to-do families in the Victorian era. The museum also has miniature shops and toy theatres.

Penshurst Place Toy Museum

Among the many treasures at Penshurst Place in Kent, the seat of the Sidney family for 450 years, is the toy museum opened in 1970 by William Sidney, the 1st Viscount de Lisle. A highlight of the museum is the Victorian dolls' house, an impressive three-storey house in red brick with contrasting white window frames and porticoed front door. Inside, the family rooms are lavishly furnished, and there is a small bathroom and the family chapel. The house has been well preserved, suggesting it was an adult showpiece rather than a toy.

Calke Abbey

A fascinating survival from the golden age of English country houses, Calke Abbey was for many years the seat of the Harpur family, known for their hoarding instincts. When the National Trust took over the property in 1985, the house was preserved as the Harpurs had left it. Among the collections is a three-storey dolls' house dating from 1860. There are six rooms and a central staircase, and the entire front opens for easy access. The house was probably played with by the four daughters of Sir Vauncey Harpur Crewe, the 10th baronet, but it has been well looked after and its homely furniture and decor reflect comfortable living.

Chapter 5

Edwardian Elegance to Modern Britain

'I want to be something so much worthier than the doll in the doll's house.'

Charles Dickens, *Our Mutual Friend*
(Chapman & Hull, 1865)

The death of Queen Victoria in 1901 put Edward VII on the throne, heralding a decade of opulence and self-indulgence among royalty and the aristocracy. But huge changes were on the horizon: two world wars loomed, and there would be four monarchs during the first half of the century before Queen Elizabeth II began her long reign in 1952. Women and the working classes were demanding greater equality in society in a direct challenge to centuries of male and upper class domination. The heyday of the English country house, with its dependence on servants, was in decline. Yet the period in between the wars, despite the Great Depression of the 1930s, was generally one of carefree gaiety: this was the age of jazz, the Charleston and Art Deco.

Dolls' houses of the period reflected emerging architectural styles, most notably the Tudor revivalism that had begun during the late nineteenth century as a backlash against Victorian Gothic architecture and developed in the twentieth century by leading architects such as Sir Edwin Lutyens (1869-1944), Mackay Hugh Baillie Scott (1865-1945) and Blair Imrie (1885-1952). A revival of Sir Christopher Wren's English Baroque style was also popular, becoming known as 'Wrenaissance'.

Significantly, dolls' house production from the beginning of the century signalled another shift in attitudes to childhood, with miniature houses and furniture now being designed with children, rather than adults, in mind. Nevertheless, collecting miniatures remained popular among adults, no doubt inspired by the creation of Queen Mary's magnificent dolls' house in the 1920s.

Toy production more or less ceased during the Second World War, but post-war Britain saw the emergence of companies such as A. Barton and the Swedish firm Lundby, dolls' house kits became increasingly popular and people have become progressively more inventive in designing and finding new purposes for miniature houses.

Early Twentieth Century

The commercial production of dolls' houses that had started in the nineteenth century became the driving force behind toy production throughout much of the twentieth century. German toymakers were still ahead of the field at the turn of the century, but that changed with the outbreak of the First World War in 1914, and many significant UK designers and makers emerged during the 1920s and '30s. Their products were competitively priced and therefore more accessible than ever, and reflected contemporary tastes in wallpaper, curtains and other furnishings. Dolls' house production was soon largely in the hands of these commercial manufacturers, making it very difficult for independent toymakers to survive.

It was three very special hand-crafted dolls' houses, though, that snatched the headlines in the early years of the twentieth century, and they introduced what seems to have been a new concept in the miniatures world – displaying dolls' houses for charitable purposes.

Sir Nevile Wilkinson's Miniature Palaces

Pembroke Palace

In 1903, Sir Nevile Wilkinson (1869–1940) – war hero, herald, writer and artist – married Lady Beatrix Herbert (1878–1957), eldest daughter of Sidney Herbert, the 14th Earl of Pembroke. The Pembroke country seat was Wilton House, a vision of Palladian splendour set in a 46,000-acre estate near Salisbury Plain. Both Wilton House and the Pembroke family history are very much at the heart of Sir Nevile's first miniature, Pembroke Palace, which replicates much of the interior décor and the collection of paintings and family portraits for which Wilton House is famous.

The three-storey dolls' house dates from 1907 and represents a typical aristocratic family in the nineteenth century, with Victorian-costumed dolls set against a backdrop of Jacobean and Georgian grandeur. Much of it was the work of craftsmen in Dublin, where Sir Nevile and Lady Beatrix lived after their marriage, but Sir Nevile was responsible for the Dining Room, Main Hall and Double Cube room. These are based on rooms at Wilton House and reflect their mid-seventeenth century Inigo Jones interiors and later Georgian modifications.

Sir Nevile's artistic skills are in evidence, too, in the three miniature family portraits in the Double Cube room. These original artworks depict his father-in-law, the 14th Earl of Pembroke, his daughter Gwendolen and a picture of himself in his official robes as Ulster King of Arms. These were clearly later additions as they are signed by Sir Nevile and dated 1911.

Pembroke Palace was exhibited at Wilton House in 1908, but then became a plaything for generations of Pembroke children before falling into disuse and ending up in a dilapidated state with much of the original furniture missing. A rescue operation in the early 1980s, overseen by London dolls' house shop The Singing Tree, saw the palace brought back to life by Uxbridge craftsman John Stevens, at a cost of £6,000.

During the six-month project, Stevens carefully restored Sir Nevile's work, but stamped his own mark on the house with authentic-looking recreations of Wilton House's interiors that sit sympathetically alongside the originals. The result is testament to Stevens' craftsmanship skills and his ambition to create a house of eye-catching splendour. Stevens was imaginative in his use of materials, and his work includes the addition of chandeliers and wall lights made with bulbs from computers and copper pots in the kitchen made from twentieth-century plumbing pipes.

Artist Bobbie Simmons was responsible for the painted ceilings in the Double Cube room and Dining Room, and for the miniature replicas of paintings in Wilton House, most notably the portraits that represent members of the Pembroke family from the time of the first Earl in the sixteenth century. The largest and most splendid is a section from a portrait of Philip, 4th Earl of Pembroke, and his family, the original of which was painted by Sir Anthony Van Dyck (1599–1641) in 1634–5 and appears in the Double Cube Room at Wilton House.

The bed linen and towels in the dolls' house were made by local craftswoman Muriel Lemon, who painstakingly embroidered the Earl of Pembroke's monogram on the hand towels, and there are further local links in the Wilton carpets in the Double Cube room and Dining Room, donated by Wilton Fabrics and Carpets.

The inclusion of Wilton carpets in the dolls' house is a nod to the Pembroke family's involvement in this world-famous industry. Thomas Herbert, the 8th Earl of Pembroke, founded the Wilton Carpet Factory in the town in the early eighteenth century, bringing Huguenot weavers over from the Savonnerie factory in Paris to pass on their skills to local weavers. By the early 20th century the company was struggling against increasing overseas competition, and this time it was Sir Nevile's father-in-law, the 14th Earl of Pembroke, who played a prominent role in saving the company by helping to establish the Wilton Royal Carpet Factory in 1904. After a somewhat chequered path through the twentieth century, including several changes of ownership, the company now exists as The Wilton Carpet Factory Ltd.

The restored Pembroke Palace was officially opened to the public on 26 March 1982 by Vivien Greene, then Lady Patron of the Dolls' House Society, and is now on permanent display by the shop entrance at Wilton House.

Titania's Palace

Long before the last Pembroke Palace nail was tapped into place, Sir Nevile had already turned his attention to a much larger and more ambitious project. The enchanting, Palladian-style Titania's Palace took fifteen years to complete and was a response to Sir Nevile's 3-year-old daughter Gwendolen, who wanted a suitable dwelling for the fairies she was convinced she had seen flitting around the garden of Mount Merrion, the family's Dublin home.

But Titania's Palace wasn't intended as a plaything. It had a nobler aim: to become a touring exhibit to raise money for charity. Both Sir Nevile and his wife were keen supporters of children's charities – Sir Nevile once served as Chairman of The League of Pity (forerunner of the NSPCC) and Lady Beatrix as President of The Children's Union (later merged into The Children's Society) – and Titania's Palace became a fundraiser for a range of local, national and international charities caring for sick and vulnerable children.

It was certainly worth exhibiting. Like the earliest dolls' houses, it was designed as a showpiece: it was intended to impress, to surprise, to enthral and to entertain. From its rich mahogany exterior and stained glass windows to the miniature treasures within, it was an exquisite masterpiece, the result of a magnificent combined effort by Sir Nevile and a team of Irish craftsmen. Sir Nevile gradually filled the palace with more than 4,000 precious objects, some believed to be around 2–3,000 years old. Some were specially made, including Sir Nevile's own miniature mosaics, and the eye-catching belfry was modelled on that of St George's Church in Hanover Square, London, by leading twentieth-century architect Sir Edwin Lutyens.

Titania's Palace was officially opened on 6 July 1922 by Queen Mary at the Daily Express Women's Exhibition, Olympia, and for the next thirty-five years the palace was exhibited all over the world, raising an estimated £150,000 for charity and attracting over 2 million viewers – including, in Los Angeles, silent movie star Charlie Chaplin.

A British Pathé film from 1933 gives a close-up of the tiny visitors' book, 'signed by Her Majesty the Queen', and shows Sir Nevile demonstrating the working parts of the 'world's smallest organ'.

In all, Titania's Palace travelled to the USA, Canada, Australia, New Zealand, Argentina and the Netherlands, as well as the length and breadth of the UK.

Sir Nevile also wrote two books to help promote Titania's Palace: *Yvette in Italy and Titania's Palace* (Humphrey Milford OUP, 1922) and *Yvette in the USA with Titania's Palace* (Nisbet & Co, 1930). Both are now out of print, but second-hand copies come up occasionally on Amazon, Ebay or similar.

Sir Nevile died in 1940, but Lady Beatrix and Gwendolen Wilkinson continued to exhibit Titania's Palace until Lady Beatrix's death in 1957. In 1967, Gwendolen put it up for auction with Christie's, with proceeds going to children's charities. The new owner, Olive Hodgkinson, displayed the palace at Wookey Hole in Somerset, where it attracted up to 60,000 visitors a year, and later at her home in St Helier, Jersey, until her death in 1977.

In January 1978, Titania's Palace was again auctioned by Christie's, where it was sold for £131,000 to Legoland and put on display in Denmark. In 2006, it was moved to its current home of Egeskov Castle in Denmark, where it is still on display to the public.

Queen Mary's Dolls' House

One of the great creative triumphs of the early twentieth century, Queen Mary's Dolls' House is a glorious edifice that brings together all that was best about Britain at the time in one magnificent package.

The house was conceived in 1921 as a gift for Queen Mary, King George V's consort and a well-known miniatures enthusiast, and took three years to complete. It was designed by Sir Edwin Lutyens at the invitation of Princess Marie Louise, a cousin of George V. Unlike Titania's Palace, with its collection of antiques, every piece in Queen Mary's dolls' house was specially commissioned, resulting in a dazzling display of contemporary British talent and enterprise.

In 1924 the dolls' house was a centrepiece at the British Empire Exhibition of Arts and Manufacturing at Wembley Park, giving a war-weary nation a much needed affirmation of everything that was good about Britain and re-establishing the country as a trading nation on the world stage. More than 1.5 million people came to see it during the seven months it was on display, and it was hailed by *The Times* as 'a miracle in miniature'. The following year it was displayed at the Ideal Home Exhibition at Olympia to raise money for the Queen's charitable fund, before being put on permanent display at Windsor Castle.

Lutyens' vision with the dolls' house was to create a detailed illustration of life in a royal residence in the early twentieth century. His four-storey Palladian-style villa was built in 1/12 scale; inside, all the main rooms are luxuriously decorated and furnished, the servants' quarters suitably downplayed but still exquisitely detailed. Everything in the house works, from the running water, electric lighting and lifts to the gramophone and the real wine in the cellar. Well-known brands of the day are featured 'below stairs', including Colman's mustard, Lea & Perrins Worcestershire Sauce, Lux flakes and Sunlight soap. The garage houses luxury cars popular at the time, including a Rolls Royce (founded 1904) and Lanchester (founded 1895), and a Rudge motorcycle (founded 1911). The garden was the work of Gertrude Jekyll, one of the leading garden designers of the day, who also contributed a miniature book, *The Garden*, to the dolls' house library.

With over 1,500 people involved, the dolls' house became a showcase for some of the finest and most popular designers, manufacturers, craftsmen, artists, writers and composers of the day. Just about everybody who was anybody at the time, it seemed, became part of this immense national project. Well, almost everyone. There were some notable dissenters: George Bernard Shaw 'wrote in a very rude manner', according to Princess Marie Louise, in turning down her invitation to contribute to the library. Sir Edward Elgar, in the words of his friend Siegfried Sassoon, was outraged that the king and queen had 'never asked for the full score of my second symphony to be added to the library at Windsor … But I'm asked to contribute to a Dolls' House for the Queen! … I consider it an insult for an artist to be asked to mix himself up in such nonsense'. John Masefield and Virginia Woolf also refused to be involved.

Nevertheless, the list of those who did contribute reads a bit like a Who's Who of 1920s' Britain. One of the most eye-catching rooms in the house is the library, which includes tiny, handwritten works by writers such as J.M. Barrie, Hilaire Belloc, John Buchan, Thomas Hardy, Rudyard Kipling and A.A. Milne.

Replicas of some of these miniatures have recently been published, including Sir Arthur Conan Doyle's *How Watson Learned the Trick*, Vita Sackville-West's *A Note of Explanation* and *J. Smith* by 'Fougasse' (real name Cyril Kenneth Bird, cartoonist and *Punch* editor from 1949–53), allowing these stories to be read for the first time, nearly 100 years after they were written.

Several composers contributed musical scores, including Arnold Bax, Frederick Delius, Gustav Holst, John Ireland, Sir Hubert Parry, Roger Quilter and Dame Ethel Smyth, while paintings by artists such as Edmund Dulac, Dame Laura Knight, Sir Alfred Munnings, Sir William Nicholson and Sir William Russell Flint are on display.

Not all contributors were household names, though. Basket-weaver Charles Brampton, who had followed in the footsteps of his father and grandfather in producing a huge range of basket ware, made a wastepaper basket for the dolls' house. Alfred Doncaster, maker of tennis rackets for Wimbledon stars and royalty, made the miniature rackets. Artist Hubert Leslie made two tiny lino cuts, while water-colourist Noel H. Leaver, who went on to gain a world-wide reputation, contributed a selection of drawings.

A major fascination of Queen Mary's dolls' house today is that by exploring its contents, we can see what people in the 1920s were reading, what music they enjoyed listening to, which artists they favoured, what they were eating and drinking, and much more besides. This is not just a dolls' house; this is a vivid slice of social history, a visual statement on Britain in the 1920s.

Mass Production

Several important manufacturers of dolls' houses and dolls' house furniture emerged during and after the First World War, when German imports ceased. There was a growing tendency towards simple designs, bright colours and the use of robust materials that were suitable for children. Between them, these pioneering manufacturers of the early twentieth century paved the way for more child-friendly dolls' houses that had instant appeal with their bright colours, encouraged use of the imagination and were suitable for small hands.

Triang

The leader of the pack for many years, Triang began life as G&J Lines Ltd in 1876, when it was formed by brothers Joseph and George. Three of Joseph's four sons, William, Walter and Arthur, joined the family firm straight from school, but broke away after the war to form their own company following disagreements about management and designs.

Lines Brothers Ltd was formally established in 1919, operating from a factory in Old Kent Road, London, and trading under the brand name Triangtois (the three lines of a triangle representing the three Lines brothers). The name was later shortened to Triang.

The new company became successful very quickly. Investment in modern machinery resulted in a production rate that far outstripped that of its competitors while still maintaining a high quality. Walter Lines designed the earliest toys made by the company, and later designed its first purpose-built factory in Morden Road, South London, which opened in 1924. By this time the company had around 500 employees, which more than doubled over the next decade.

The range of Triang dolls' houses grew rapidly, varying in size and style from simple thatched cottages to country mansions and Art Deco-style houses. They changed little over the years, the basic design being carefully replicated or adapted. During the 1920s and '30s, Walter tapped into the vogue for Tudor revivalism by producing dolls' houses with mock-Tudor exteriors, reproducing the gabled roofs, half-timbering, ornate balustrades and mullioned or oriel windows that were characteristic of the style. This became one of Triang's most popular ranges.

Walter also ensured that Triang houses were suitable for children. As such, they tended to be brightly coloured, often with flowers painted on the front for added appeal, and they had either hinged front-opening doors or sliding fronts for maximum access. Triang's slogan was 'Simply made and beautifully coloured', and this can be seen in the many surviving Triang houses.

One of Triang's most famous dolls' houses is Princess Elizabeth's Little House, which was modelled on Y Bwthyn Bach ('The Little Cottage'), a thatched playhouse made in Cardiff by local craftsmen and presented to Princess Elizabeth in April 1932 to mark her sixth birthday. The young princess had to wait until December to play in the house though, as it was displayed at the Daily Mail Ideal Home Exhibition to raise money for children's charities before being transported back to the Royal Lodge at Windsor, where it remains today.

Y Bwthyn Bach was immensely popular, so Walter Lines designed a miniature version and it became one of Triang's best-selling models. It was produced from the 1930s to the 1950s, and appeared in many different versions. The V&A Museum of Childhood and the Museum of Childhood in

Edinburgh both have versions of the house; the latter also has a copy of the official guide book issued when the original dolls' house was exhibited in 1932.

Lanhydrock in Cornwall and the Museum of Childhood at Sudbury Hall both feature one of Triang's grander designs: a white, twin-gabled, three-storey Edwardian-style villa from the early 1900s, fully furnished. The museum at Sudbury Hall has other Triang models too, including one of the 1930s mock-Tudor range. The displays at Ilkley Toy Museum include Sunnyside, a three-storey house with metal-framed windows and 1930s furniture, while Hove Museum and Art Gallery has Purvis House, another 1930s model with garage, electric wall lights and original fireplaces.

Other early twentieth century manufacturers

The Lines brothers may have dominated the toy manufacturing scene, but other firms were making their mark too. Amersham Toy Company produced a wide range of soft toys and wooden goods in the town from 1924, including dolls' houses and dolls' house furniture. Their dolls' houses were typically mock-Tudor, not unlike the Triang range, with timbering, gables and flowers painted on the front, and uniquely featured tin windows. Larger models included a garage. Furniture was simple but tasteful in its design, and ideal for children to handle. The factory closed in 1960 when production was transferred to Wales, but you can see a display of Amersham toys, including a dolls' house, at Amersham Museum.

The Dereham-based Hobbies was started in 1895 by John Skinner and became very successful during the early twentieth century, selling dolls' house kits, furniture, accessories and tools to budding model makers. Styles reflected contemporary architecture and furnishings, although Georgian- and Victorian-style houses were added later. In 1907 Hobbies successfully sued rival company Handicrafts, started by John's brother Frank, for poaching its designs and customer mailing list. Hobbies closed in 1968 after being taken over by Great Universal Stores. Its weekly magazine, which had been running since the company started, ceased publication, but its annual catalogue still exists. Bishop Bonner's Cottage Museum in Dereham has a display of Hobbies memorabilia, donated in 2017.

Tinplate toys were popular in the early twentieth century, produced by toolmakers A.S. Cartwright from 1905 and Wells-Brimtoy – formed from the merger of Alfred Wells and British Metal and Toy Manufacturers Ltd (BRIMTOY) in the 1930s – whose most popular product, from the 1950s, was My Dolly's Kitchen, a range of cream and red tinplate kitchen furniture. Mettoy was established in Northampton in 1933 by Philip Ullmann and Arthur Katz and made a range of tinplate toys, including dolls' houses. Taylor & Barrett, established in 1920, parted ways to form two separate companies in 1945, with F.G. Taylor & Sons producing gas and electric cookers and A. Barrett & Sons (Toys) Ltd specialising in kitchen tools and accessories.

Elgin of Enfield Ltd produced wooden furniture from 1919 and counted Queen Mary among its customers. The company was taken over by Lines Brothers in 1926. A little later on the scene was Dol-Toi Products Ltd., established in 1944 and specialising in miniature household accessories.

Child-friendly dolls' houses

Among those moving towards more child-friendly dolls' houses, manufacturers Paul and Marjorie Abbatt were hugely influential. Toymaker Marjorie Cobb (1899–1991) and teacher Paul Abbatt (1899–1971) met in 1926 and quickly discovered a shared interest in the value of learning through play. They married in 1930, and two years later, encouraged by their visits to progressive schools in Vienna, established Paul and Marjorie Abbatt Ltd to make and sell toys that were both functional and educational.

Initially operating as a mail-order business, the Abbatts opened a showroom at Endsleigh Street in 1934, designed for them by Hungarian architect and furniture designer Ernö Goldfinger (1902–1987), a pioneer of the modernist movement. It was the beginning of a fruitful partnership between the Abbatts and Goldfinger, who collaborated on displays for the Contemporary Industrial Design Exhibition in London in 1934 and for the British Pavilion at the Paris Exhibition in 1937.

In 1936 Goldfinger designed the frontage, interior, furniture and some of the toys for the Abbatts' new shop at Wimpole Street, London. This ground-breaking toy wonderland was designed to be child-friendly, a place where everything was easily accessible and children were allowed to touch. Toys were in primary colours and shaped for small hands. Dolls' houses came in bright, simple designs, with roofs that lifted off and sides that opened so that children could easily explore the interiors.

In *Play and Toys* (1957), Paul Abbatt wrote: 'Their hands must have easy access to the interior of the dolls' house so that they may arrange and rearrange the furniture and imagine themselves in charge of all domestic affairs.'

Meanwhile, Goldfinger's toymaking skills were put to use in his own home. When his daughter, Liz, wanted a dolls' house for Christmas he happily obliged – only for Liz to burst into tears when she saw what he had given her! It's not surprising: the rectangular, roofless modern bungalow, built in dark plywood, is stark and uninviting, with a few contents that are out of proportion and not in keeping with the style of the house. It is now on display at 2 Willow Road, Hampstead, the house that Goldfinger designed and lived in with his family from 1939 until his death in 1987.

Second World War

General shortages during the Second World War, and the need to divert any essential materials towards the war effort, meant that commercial toy manufacture more or less ceased until after the war. Toys quickly became rare as toy factories, such as Mettoy and Lines Brothers, turned to producing war-related goods. The 'make do and mend' mantra on the home front spilled over into toymaking, and people became quite ingenious at fashioning dolls' houses and their contents from scraps of material and other objects that would otherwise have been thrown away, such as matchboxes, matchsticks, fir cones, feathers, clothes pegs, seed pods, pins and string. The Irene Cornelius dolls' house collection, formerly at Bletchley Park, included furniture sets made from card and covered in cloth or wallpaper, as well as a very distinctive set of furniture made with pins pushed into corks with green silk wound around the pins.

One of the most interesting examples of a privately made dolls' house from the war years is Spitfire Cottage, made by sisters Philippa Miller and Pamela Baker while on fire-watching duties at Blyth School (now Sewell Park Academy) on the outskirts of Norwich. The 1/12 scale house has four rooms, two up and two down, with no staircase. It was constructed entirely from cardboard and furnished with scraps of material and any other odds and ends they could lay their hands on. The upper floor sags slightly and the walls are not quite straight, but that adds to the charm and very personal touch of this authentic Second World War relic. The sisters exhibited the house during the war and helped raise £40 towards the cost of building a Spitfire. The dolls' house is now in the collection of the Museum of Norwich at the Bridewell.

Another house from this era is Thelma's House, which is on display at the Jewish Museum in London. Built in the modernist style by Malcolm Libling, the son of an East End furniture maker, for his daughter Thelma, it reflects the aspirations of Britain's Jewish community before, during and immediately after the war, when they were mostly living in cramped conditions in London's East End. The dolls' house was based on a real house in the seaside town of Angmering-on-Sea in West Sussex, and is a pleasantly light house with two large windows, a first floor balcony and simple porticoed front door. It looks in good condition, suggesting that the young Thelma regarded it as something to admire rather than as a plaything.

Sheffield Museums collections include a set of dolls' house furniture made during the war by an Italian prisoner of war at the Lodge Moor POW camp near Redmires Reservoirs, Sheffield. The furniture was presented to a local lady, Mrs Doris Taylor, who often walked by the camp with her son.

Post-War Britain

Toy production for many firms continued after the war. Lines Brothers opened new factories in Merthyr Tydfil and Belfast, and the company once again dominated the market, both home and abroad, as it scooped up ownership of numerous other companies including Meccano, Hornby and Dinky. In its heyday, Lines Brothers had around forty companies worldwide, producing a huge range of dolls' houses, soldiers, Noah's Ark, soft toys, model cars and much more. The company's luck finally ran out in 1971 when the failure of its overseas ventures forced it into liquidation.

By this time, other designers and manufacturers were already jostling to take its place, many of them keen to tap into the new trend for child-friendly toys. Italian sculptor Antonio Vitali started making toys in 1946, including a range of dolls' house furniture that was smoothly shaped to make it easy for small hands to grasp. Mettoy, which had moved to Wales during the war, resumed production of its tinplate range, and began producing plastic goods from 1948.

A. Barton & Co (Toys) Ltd started up just after the war making 1/16 scale accessories for dolls' houses, including fireplaces, electric 'bar' fires, wooden 'wireless' radios, grandfather clocks and box televisions in cabinets. The use of plastics increased after the war, and Barton produced a range of plastic accessories for dolls' houses. These were ideal for children as they were washable and unbreakable, making them both sturdy and hygienic. One of the company's most popular products was Caroline's House, which made its debut in 1957 and was a light, airy house filled with brightly coloured plastic furniture.

In 1984 Barton was sold to Swedish firm Lundby, which had been established in Lundby, near Gothenberg, in 1945 by Axel and Grete Thomsen. The clean lines and stylish furniture, reflecting contemporary tastes, were a hit with young dolls' house enthusiasts, as was their decision to continue producing Caroline's House when they took over Barton. A Lundby house from the 1970s is on display at the Museum of Childhood at Sudbury Hall.

Popular firms to emerge during the late twentieth century include Bluebird Toys (1980) with their distinctive yellow teapot house and Polly Pocket (1980s) and its range of miniature homes. Dolls' house kits have become the vogue, the most notable manufacturer of the post-war years being the Dolls House Emporium, which began by selling 1/24 scale kits by mail order before expanding to produce a wide range of dolls' house kits, dolls' houses, dolls' house furniture and accessories. Over the years, the company has had particular success with its houses modelled on popular architectural styles, from Georgian to Art Deco.

Home-made houses also remained popular after the war. The need to improvise during the war instilled in people a self-sufficiency that continued in the post-war years, and many home-made dolls' houses appeared in British homes during the 1950s and 1960s.

Now, in the twenty-first century, the passion for dolls' houses and all things miniature seems to be as strong as ever, and some delightfully quirky examples have emerged over the last few years. Just outside Chipping Norton in Oxfordshire, for example, is Mouse Town, a beautifully crafted indoor model village that was originally made for a travelling circus but was obtained by visitor attraction Fairytale Farm in 2014. After extensive restoration, it is now home to a family of around fifteen mice.

Built during the 1990s, this charming model resembles a medieval village with its timber-framed buildings, gabled roofs, bay windows and Narnia-like lamp posts. The focal point is the village green with its duck pond and stocks, while to the right is a church with a slender spire and tiny graveyard. At Christmas the town is decorated with fake snow. Its tiny residents live behind the model, but at times during the day they can be seen scampering in and out of the model buildings.

More recently, a woolly version of Thrapston in Northamptonshire appeared when a group of ladies known as the Yarn Bombers knitted their way into the history books with models of some of the town's most notable buildings, including the eighteenth-century pub, church, cinema, post office and several local shops and businesses. These incredibly detailed and accurate woolly recreations included tiny poppies in an area of remembrance, fruit and vegetables on a high street stall, and several woolly figures going about their daily business. The town was two years in the making and was displayed in the local church during the annual arts festival to raise money for the church roof.

In October 2019 several national newspapers reported that London-based actor Jon Trenchard had spent thirty years creating a miniature stately home, Hordle Castle, which was inspired by childhood visits to various National Trust properties. From creating a single room at the age of 12, he now has eight rooms, filled with hand-crafted or readymade furniture, soft furnishings, ornaments and other domestic objects. In keeping with the environmentally aware age, much of the house and its contents have been fashioned from recycled materials, including cereal packets and egg boxes. Now he has plans to create further rooms and to write a National Trust-style guidebook.

Dolls' houses for all

The twenty-first century has seen a growing trend for community dolls' house projects, from those involving experienced or aspiring miniaturists to those giving a voice to marginalised groups of people.

At Upton House, a National Trust property on the Oxfordshire-Warwickshire border, volunteers from all over the world spent sixteen months recreating the house as it looked in the 1930s when it belonged to Lord and Lady Bearsted, the final owners before the National Trust acquired the property in 1948.

The 'Made-to-Measure' project was a tribute to the craftsmanship and vision of Lord and Lady Bearsted, who turned the house into a showcase for Lord Bearsted's collections of art and porcelain. Lady Bearsted, an interior designer with an eye on the latest fashions, created a startling Art Deco bathroom and, by contrast, an eighteenth-century style bedroom with a four-poster bed and a chinoiserie cabinet. Much of this was recreated in miniature in the dolls' house.

The model – a representation of the house rather than an exact replica – was built in 1/12 scale by craftsman Bob Packer, and the National Trust then invited volunteers from the local community and beyond to contribute handmade fittings, furnishings and domestic items typical of the late 1920s and early 1930s. Around ninety volunteers became involved in the project, including three people in America, one in Ireland and others from all over the UK.

The dolls' house was on temporary display at Upton until spring 2020, but there are plans to create room boxes for the miniatures and use them to complement the displays in the real house.

Another recent National Trust project, at The Workhouse, Southwell, put a dolls' house at the centre of an art installation involving young women from Newark Emmaus Trust. The installation, simply named 'Nesting', was the outcome of a series of workshops led by artist

Natalie L. Mann exploring issues of homelessness among young parents. The setting of the installation, the recently restored Firbeck Infirmary at Southwell Workhouse, gave the project a particular resonance.

Similar issues were explored by the V&A Museum of Childhood in June 2019 when refugees, schoolchildren and volunteers were invited to contribute individual room boxes to create a giant dolls' house reflecting problems faced by refugees. Each of the room boxes – more than a hundred in total – told a unique story: some aspirational, some shocking, but all poignant.

Into the future

What a long way dolls' houses have come in 400 years. From adult showpieces, they have become playthings for generations of children. They have also once again become collectables for adults, but their appeal now is less to do with status symbols and more to do with a genuine fascination for miniatures and what they can tell us about our past. And finally, from being a vehicle for boasting of wealth and privilege, they are being used to amplify voices that need to be heard. Now, it seems, dolls' houses are for everyone: something truly universal.

Chapter 6

Recreating The Past

'Escapism? Oh, yes. But then we all need a bit of that from time to time.'

Alan Titchmarsh, 'Dolls' houses are perfect miniature worlds' *The Telegraph* February 15, 2014

There's nothing quite like looking at historical dolls' houses that have survived to the modern day. Such houses are genuine relics of the past and give us a connection to the people who created them and those that owned and cared for them. But there has been a trend from the early twentieth century onwards to recreate the past with meticulously researched dolls' houses that also give us a glimpse into a bygone era. Some are based on real buildings, in some cases ones that no longer exist. Often they have strong links to their local area, and some pioneered the idea of creating dolls' houses as community projects – an idea that has gained traction during the twenty-first century (see Chapter 5).

Miniature Model Houses at Hever Castle

This outstanding collection of miniatures, housed at the childhood home of Anne Boleyn, illustrates in 1/12 scale the architecture and domestic life of the English country house from the Tudors to the Victorians, thereby taking the viewer on an authentically recreated journey through time. As there are no surviving dolls' houses from before the late seventeenth century, this is a rare opportunity to see earlier periods captured in miniature.

The collection was commissioned in 1989 by John Guthrie, owner of Hever Castle, and built by leading English miniaturist and painter John J. Hodgson, with contributions from many other leading artists and miniaturists. It took ten years to complete, and replicates in extraordinary detail many of the features found at Hever Castle and in other great country houses around England. All the houses are populated by realistic-looking figures made from putty and dressed in period costume.

The *Medieval House* includes a great hall, a solar (the master's bedchamber) and a kitchen. The great hall was modelled on the one at nearby Penshurst Place, a fourteenth-century manor house once owned by Henry VIII, but the stained glass window designs are based on those at Hever Castle. The ceiling, rafters and furniture were all carved from seventeenth-century oak, and a tapestry depicting Henry VIII and Anne Boleyn was crafted on antique silk by dolls' house collector Patricia Borwick and contains over 42,000 tiny stitches.

The solar features silk bed linen, a beautifully illustrated Psalter with readable words, and a lute made from mahogany, ebony and spruce. The carpet was inspired by the Ardabil Carpet, which originated in Persia in 1540 and is one of the

A Georgian dolls' house on display at Amersham Museum. © Nicola Lisle; reproduced with kind permission of Amersham Museum.

Darley Hall, an early Victorian dolls' house at Blaise Castle House Museum. © Nicola Lisle; reproduced by kind permission of the museum.

(*Above*) Carpenter-made house from the Buckinghamshire County Museum collections. Picture supplied by the museum and reproduced with their kind permission.

(*Below*) German kitchen at Ilkley Toy Museum. © Nicola Lisle; reproduced with kind permission of the museum.

(*Above*) Butcher's shop at Old House Museum, Bakewell. © Nicola Lisle; reproduced by kind permission of the museum.

(*Below*) Butcher's shop at Museum of Childhood, Edinburgh. © Nicola Lisle; reproduced by kind permission of the museum.

(*Above and opposite above*) Stanbrig Eorls at the Museum of Childhood, Edinburgh. © Nicola Lisle; reproduced by kind permission of the museum.

(*Opposite below*) Victorian dolls' house in the toy museum at Penshurst Place. Picture supplied by Penshurst and reproduced by kind permission of Viscount De L'Isle and the Penshurst Place estate.

(*Above and left*) Pembroke Palace general view and first floor landing – © Nicola Lisle; reproduced by kind permission of the 18th Earl of Pembroke and Trustees of the Wilton Estate.

1930s Tudor-style dolls' house by Triang at the Museum of Childhood, Edinburgh. © Nicola Lisle; reproduced by kind permission of the museum.

(*Above*) Triang's Y Bwythn Bach at the Museum of Childhood, Edinburgh. © Nicola Lisle; reproduced by kind permission of the museum.

(*Below left*) Dolls' house by Amersham Toy Company, on display at Amersham Museum. Picture supplied by the museum and reproduced with their kind permission.

(*Below right*) Dolls' house at the heart of the 'Nesting' project at The Workhouse, Southwell. © Nicola Lisle; reproduced by kind permission of Dr Natalie J. Mann and The National Trust/Southwell Workhouse.

Miniature model house collection at Hever Castle. Pictures supplied by Hever Castle and reproduced with their kind permission.

Main hall of the Medieval house.

Elizabethan house.

Restoration Stuart room.

Main hall of the
Georgian house.

Dining room of the
Georgian house.

Victorian parlour.

(*Above*) Part of the Carlisle Collection at Nunnington Hall. © Nicola Lisle; reproduced by kind permission of The National Trust.

(*Below left*) Dolls' house at Overbeck's. © Nicola Lisle; reproduced by kind permission of The National Trust.

(*Below right and opposite above*) Dolls' house at the Tolsey Museum, Burford. © Nicola Lisle; reproduced by kind permission of the museum.

(*Above left and above right*) Dolls' house modelled on Charles Dickens' house at Doughty Street, London. © Nicola Lisle; reproduced by kind permission of the museum.

(*Left*) Exterior of the real
Charles Dickens house at
Doughty Street. © Nicola Lisle.

(*Below*) Havercroft
Mackenzie house at Greys
Court., Henley-on-Thames.
© Nicola Lisle; reproduced
by kind permission of
The National Trust.

Bekonscot Model Village. © Nicola Lisle; reproduced by kind permission of Bekonscot Model Village.

(*Above and right*) Model of Greenacres, Enid Blyton's former home, with plaque.

(*Below left*) Harbour.

(*Below right*) Cover of brochure from the 1930s.

GREEN HEDGES
The home of Enid Blyton in Beaconsfield from 1938 - 1968.
This replica was presented by the Mayor (Councillor Mrs Margaret Dewar) and Town Council of Beaconsfield, and unveiled by Mrs Gillian Baverstock – elder daughter of Enid Blyton – on the 6th April, 1997 in the year of the Author's Centenary.

BEKONSCOT
MODEL RAILWAY AND VILLAGE
WARWICK ROAD
BEACONSFIELD
(Three Minutes from Station)

(By permission of the London "Evening News")

OPEN EVERY SUNDAY
(APRIL TO SEPTEMBER)
2 p.m. TO DUSK

Admission - - - 1/-
(Children Half-price)

Proceeds in aid of the funds of
RAILWAY BENEVOLENT INSTITUTION AND
QUEEN'S INSTITUTE OF DISTRICT NURSING
The Village is also open on
TUESDAY, THURSDAY & SATURDAY AFTERNOONS
(Model Trains not working)

(*Left and below*) Part of the Beryl Dade Dolls' House Collection on display at Wimborne Model Town. © Nicola Lisle; reproduced by kind permission of Wimborne Model Town.

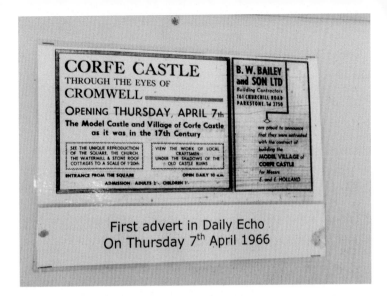

First advert in Daily Echo
On Thursday 7th April 1966

Corfe Castle Model Village. © Nicola Lisle; reproduced by kind permission of the model village.

Whiteway at Saltram, originally part of Vivien Greene's collection. © Nicola Lisle; reproduced by kind permission of The National Trust.

Saltram House, Devon, possibly the model for Whiteway. © Nicola Lisle.

Old Original Swan at Ilkley Toy Museum, originally part of Vivien Greene's collection. © Nicola Lisle; reproduced by kind permission of Ilkley Toy Museum.

Dolls' houses donated by Mary Greg to Manchester Art Gallery; currently in storage. © Nicola Lisle; reproduced by kind permission of Manchester Art Gallery.

oldest carpets in the world; the original, described in 1843 by William Morris as 'singular perfection ... consistently beautiful', can be seen in the Jameel Gallery at the V&A Museum in London.

The *Stuart House* is based on Burton Agnes Hall, an Elizabethan stately home in East Yorkshire. The symmetrical, E-shaped building is typical of the period, as are the elaborately carved wooden panels, decorative plasterwork on the ceilings and exquisite tapestries, all the influence of Flemish craftsmen who settled in England during the late sixteenth century after fleeing Spanish persecution.

The house provides charming snapshots of Elizabethan country house life. In the parlour, an elderly lady is at her spinning wheel, with a basket of wool from Leicester long-haired sheep at her side. In the Long Gallery, which was often used for indoor games, gentlemen are enjoying games of tennis or shovelboard, the forerunner of shove halfpenny.

Much of the furniture is based on tables and chairs at Hever Castle, and many of the portraits – all the work of Hodgson – are replicas of those at the castle.

The *Restoration Drawing Room* captures the opulence and extravagance that evolved after the restoration of the monarchy in 1660. The elaborately carved garlands of flowers and fruit that adorn the oak-panelled walls and plaster ceilings are in the style of the celebrated English woodcarver Grinling Gibbons (1648–1721), whose work appears at Windsor Castle, Hampton Court Palace, St Paul's Cathedral, Petworth House and many other English churches and stately homes. Some of the carving on the ceiling here was based on the ceiling in Hever Castle's library.

The marquetry skills of the Huguenot émigrés, who fled persecution by the French Catholics in the 1680s, are reflected in much of the furniture, including an exquisite spiral-legged walnut cabinet inlaid with ivory and a Charles II marquetry longcase clock. Chinoiserie was beginning to make an appearance in England in the seventeenth century (see Chapter 3), and there is a magnificent example here in the black Chinese lacquered cabinet with its exotic pattern and richly ornate gilt base and crested top. The William and Mary chairs, representing the more elegant style of furniture that characterised the late seventeenth century, are replicas of chairs featured in Hever Castle's Long Gallery.

The *Georgian House* is styled on Sledmere House, a Grade I listed country house in East Yorkshire. Typical Georgian elegance and grandeur abound here, from the Palladian-style staircase, marbled columns, exotic Chinese ornaments and intricately designed rugs to the rich mahogany furniture in the style of Thomas Chippendale. Each piece of the Wedgewood-style bone china dinner service in the dining room features a 'G' monogram in honour of the Guthrie family, the current owners of Hever Castle, while the set of porcelain plates displayed in an alcove at the end of the room was inspired by a design from Sudbury Hall in Derbyshire.

The *Victorian room settings* include a hallway, drawing room, nursery and kitchen, and illustrate the contrast between the wealthy family and their servants. The parlour is in the Gothic revival style popular in the late

Victorian era with its characteristic arch-shaped windows and doorways and ornamental cornice. The wallpaper is a William Morris design, 'Bower', dating from 1877, and the parquet woodblock floor is covered with a carpet inspired by the French Aubusson or Savonnerie carpets.

The room has been decorated for Christmas and includes many of the seasonal favourites first popularised by the Victorians – including, of course, the Christmas tree, introduced to Britain by Prince Albert in 1841, as well as crackers, sweets, paper chains, presents under the tree and festive garland on the mantelpiece. Carol singing was popular with the Victorians, and here the family has gathered around the piano to sing or play musical instruments. In the hallway the maid has opened the door to a group of carol singers, who traditionally would have been plied with mince pies and wassail.

The nursery is typically Victorian with its collection of mechanical and educational toys, model soldiers, hobby horses, dolls, dolls' house and books. The nanny dozing in the corner has been sewing; on a nearby table are her silk threads and a sewing machine.

In the kitchen, the gardener brings in some fresh vegetables, while the cook and maid are busily preparing the festive fare. There is a selection of meats, some freshly baked mince pies and Christmas puddings wrapped in muslin, and the kitchen is well-equipped with copper and brass pans, a vast array of cooking utensils, kitchen crockery and serving dishes, and the all-important cast-iron kitchen range.

The Carlisle Collection of Miniature Rooms, Nunnington Hall

Unlike the display at Hever Castle, which was commissioned as a specific project, the collection of miniature rooms at Nunnington Hall in Yorkshire evolved over many years and involved some of the leading craftsmen and miniaturists of the time. Between them, these rooms recreate, in exquisite detail, typical domestic settings over a period of 300 years with a mixture of genuine antiques and authentic replicas. There are no dolls, though; in the tradition of the old German and Dutch baby and cabinet houses, this collection is unashamedly a showpiece, but one that both adults and children can admire.

This magnificent display is the result of the life-long collecting habit of Mrs F.M. 'Kitty' Carlisle (1891–1979), whose interest in miniatures began as a child when she was given a set of 1/8 scale furniture pieces in filigree silver from China and India.

She began collecting in earnest during the 1920s when she was setting up her first marital home in London and wanted some miniature items to complement her silver collection. Early acquisitions were mostly furniture-makers' miniature samples, and this quickly expanded to include an assortment of domestic objects, both antique and contemporary, made from wood, china, glass, silver and ivory.

It soon became clear that she needed a cabinet to showcase her collection, and from this grew the idea of creating a series of room settings, each appropriately styled and furnished to represent a specific era. Between 1933 and 1968, Kitty commissioned some of Britain's leading craftsmen to create entire rooms or contribute specific items, instructing them to work in 1/8 scale in line with her original miniatures. Kitty's room settings were originally on display at Pyt House, her Berkshire home, and she occasionally opened the house to visitors for a small charge, with proceeds going to local and national charities.

The *William and Mary Parlour* was commissioned from Wiltshire craftsman Horace Uphill, who had made some of the furniture for Titania's Palace (see pages 66-68). The elegant table and high-backed chairs are complemented by a Dutch silver tea service, displays of Chinese figurines in the alcoves and a series of wall-mounted enamel plaques depicting lovers in rural settings. The leaf-patterned carpet was based on an original from the Savonnerie factory in Paris. There is also a wooden baby walker, similar in design to the one in the Nuremberg House at the V&A Museum of Childhood (see pages 6-7).

The furniture in the *Queen Anne Drawing Room*, the first of Kitty's commissions, was made in 1933 by cabinet-maker F.J. Early, described in the original guidebook (May 1969) as someone whose 'attention to detail and accuracy have served as a challenge to all other miniature makers'. A contributor to both Queen Mary's dolls' house and Titania's Palace, Early produced exquisitely made tables, chairs and writing bureau in walnut, all with dovetail joints, and the bureau has several secret drawers and locks with working keys.

The parana pine panelling, complemented by finely carved corner shelves and overdoor panel were the work of Albert Reeves and replaced the original setting in 1968.

Reeves also created the *Adam Music Room* in 1960, replicating the neoclassicism of Robert Adam with the delicately carved back wall inlaid with Wedgwood wall plaques and fronted by busts mounted on pedestals. Reeves also made the spinet, violin, viola and clarinet, but the largest collection of instruments – harp, cello, viola da gamba, recorders and castanets – were all made by Cardiff carpenter John Weston Thomas, who went on to become a professional harp maker. All the instruments can produce musical notes.

The *Chippendale Library* was again the work of F.J. Early, who used mahogany – the favoured wood of the late eighteenth century – to replicate the style of Thomas Chippendale. The bookcase along the right-hand wall, the desk, drumtop table and magazine rack – with copies of *Country Life* and *Reader's Digest* – make an elegant composition, and once again the standard of workmanship is impeccable.

The library contains fifty books, including an Almanack from 1770, educational books intended for Victorian nurseries, and copies of the Bible, Koran and Gita.

On the drumtop table is a visitors' book containing the signatures of most of the craftsmen involved in the entire collection. Sadly, Early had died by the time this was produced, but Kitty had his signature from one of his letters photographed and printed on the first page to ensure that this leading contributor was included.

The majestic *Palladian Hall* was based on the hall at Hatch House, Wiltshire, a late eighteenth-century house, now Grade I listed, designed by Somerset MP and amateur architect Thomas Prowse. The work of Albert Reeves, this is the only setting in the collection to be based on a real place, the inspiration having come from a *Country Life* article on Hatch House in October 1964.

The need to show both ground floor and landing necessitated a reduction in scale to 1/10, and the result is spectacular. A central pier glass at the top of the first flight of stairs incorporates an Italian mosaic of the Parthenon in Rome, and was a piece that Kitty Carlisle had owned for years before finding the perfect place to display it.

In the hallway, the stairs are flanked by a pair of torchieres (floor-standing lamps) and framed by two graceful ionic columns. The stair carpet and oval rugs in the hall and on the landing were all embroidered by Kitty Carlisle, and there are portraits of her grandchildren on the walls.

The setting for the *Georgian Bedroom* was the work of two Fulham-based craftsmen, R.J. Magna and John Moore, who were both experienced in making model replicas for commercial and official use. Magna ran his own business making furniture models for use in lectures by the Council of Industrial Design, while Moore, who joined him in 1949, had made model ships and aircraft for training purposes before the war. By the time they were recruited to work on the Carlisle Collection, they were producing model furniture samples for the High Wycombe-based furniture manufacturer Ercolani.

Several pieces in the Georgian room – a corner washstand, chest with mirror, wardrobe, round bedside table and cradle – are period pieces, and they are augmented by modern replicas, including a central Pembroke table made by John Moore and other pieces by F.J. Early, Horace Uphill and Albert Reeves.

The main fascination with this room, however, lies in the exquisite needlework. The bedspread on the four-poster bed was made by patchwork specialist Averil Colby, author of *Patchwork* (Batsford, 1958) and *Patchwork Quilts* (Batsford, 1965), and there is a set of neatly folded, hand-stitched household linen in the wardrobe. The striped petit point upholstery for the chairs and chaise longue are in keeping with the period, and there are unfinished pieces of tatting and lacework, as well as a sewing table, suggesting that the room was occupied by a keen needlewoman. The carpet design was adapted by the Royal School of Needlework from an early nineteenth-century Aubusson.

The setting for the *Regency Games Room* was designed by architect D.B. Waterhouse, ARIBA, and made by Horace Uphill, who also made most of the furniture. F.J. Early was responsible for the rather splendid Carlton House desk – a style of desk designed by George Hepplewhite in the early eighteenth century for the Prince of Wales (later George IV) and featuring a distinctive U-shaped arrangement of drawers.

The chairs – featuring similar striped upholstery to the ones in the Georgian bedroom – were made by Albert Reeve, who also made the hearth with fender and fire-irons, and the china figurines mounted on decorative wall brackets.

The miniature games were originally part of Kitty's collection and were the inspiration for this room. Around the room are various tables set up for chess, draughts, backgammon, dominoes and cards, all popular in England during the eighteenth century. The shelves either side of the fireplace contain more chess pieces as well as ninepins and boxes of dice. There are children's toys here too, including a spinning top and a cup and ball.

The inspiration for the *Victorian Picture Gallery* came from a set of watercolours in Kitty's collection. These have been augmented by prints by George Baxter (1805–1867), an English artist, engraver and printer who invented a process of oil-colour printing that enabled mass production of paintings. The pictures here were all taken from the wrappers in which sets of needles were sold.

An accumulation of miniature toys was Kitty's inspiration for the *Day Nursery*, much of which was made by R.J. Magna and John Moore using wood from a sycamore tree at Pyt House. This included a wooden play pen, table and several bookcases filled with books and toys.

Moore added the dolls' house in 1960, and was also responsible for the fort and Noah's Ark. The huge chain of ivory animals waiting to enter the ark were brought back from Rhodesia and Sudan by Kitty's son and daughter. Among them is a pair of 'mystery' animals that are clearly not part of the original set and were presumably made by a different craftsman and added at a later date.

By 1961, the day nursery was getting too crowded so the *Night Nursery* was added. Albert Reeves was largely responsible for work on this room, including the rocking horse – now in the day nursery – the swing cot, table, chairs, cupboard and shelves, as well as the brightly coloured frieze featuring cottages, boats and fish.

The furniture in the *Post-War Living Room*, added in 1949 by R.J. Magna and John Moore, was made from the wood of a pear tree in the gardens at Pyt House, and the simplicity in style and layout perfectly evoke the feel of the immediate post-war years.

The parquet floor is made up of 1,600 beechwood blocks, and the bookshelves include a complete set of the works of Shakespeare. There are some lovely personal touches in this room, including the pen drawing of Pyt House by R.J. Magna and a china model of the house by Margaret Binns. On the desk is an old-fashioned green phone and an in-tray containing tiny letters written by Kitty's four children.

The collection also includes some workshops added in 1953, containing Victorian copper tools and other tools and equipment made as working scale models by John Weston Thomas. Later additions include a greenhouse (1957), tool shed (1960) and antique shop (1962).

In 1970 Kitty presented the collection to the National Trust, and for the next ten years it was displayed at Grey's Court, near Henley-on-Thames in Oxfordshire. In 1980, a year after Kitty Carlisle's death, it was transferred to the seventeenth-century Nunnington Hall, where it remains to this day.

A few years ago, the collection was given a makeover with a completely redesigned setting. Instead of perching on plinths, as in the past, the miniature rooms were set into National Trust-type house frontages to give them a stylish, elegant new setting that shows them up to better advantage. Lighting was also added, for the first time in the collection's history, serving to highlight the details in the rooms. During the refurbishment process, all the items were carefully photographed and numbered so that they could all be returned to their original positions. Kitty Carlisle's ghost must surely be nodding in approval.

Georgian Grandeur at Overbeck's

The lovely Palladian-style dolls' house at Overbeck's in Devon was created during the 1980s by self-taught craftswoman Mabel Hill, who was inspired by the National Trust places she had visited, such as nearby Saltram and Lanhydrock in Cornwall. Although not an exact copy, there is certainly more than a hint of Saltram's Georgian splendour in the cream-coloured frontage, the symmetrically placed Palladian windows, the first floor balcony and the ornately decorated central pediment flanked by twin chimney stacks.

Inside, the house gives a well-researched snapshot of a wealthy Georgian family home. The entrance hall is elegant and restrained, a hint of the splendour to come. A grand central staircase, with decorative wooden balustrading, leads to a spacious first floor landing with paintings, a grandfather clock, wooden octagonal table and patterned rug, all carefully ordered to create a pleasing effect.

On the ground floor, the dining room is a vision of opulence with its matching red chairs and drapes, coordinated patterned rug, sparkling chandelier and candelabra. In the corner is a silver fruit tray and a few bottles of wine. The bookcase on the far wall is perhaps a nod to the fact that

Saltram's dining room was originally the library. Each of the books in the bookcase was individually handmade.

Across the hallway, the drawing room is similarly plush with deep pink drapes, marble-effect fireplace, and a piano that actually plays. The doll seated at the piano wears a typical mid-eighteenth-century, full-length dress trimmed with lace and ribbon, and her hair is pinned up and decorated with more ribbon.

The bedrooms on the first and second floors feature four-poster beds that hint at the Chippendale-style beds at Saltram, and they are lavishly decorated with richly coloured coordinating bed linen, canopy and drapes. Mahogany furniture, decorative rugs, print wallpapers, fireplaces and paintings complete the effect.

The house took a few years to make and is testament to Mabel Hill's innovation and flair. The main floors are lit with real electric lighting, the carpets, rugs and bell-pulls were all painstakingly embroidered by hand, the paintings cut from card and framed, and smaller items, such as the food in the dining room and kitchen and the vanity sets in the bedroom, were all made from modelling clay.

Many of the materials used had personal connections to Mabel and her family. Remnants of wallpaper from the family home were pressed into service in the dolls' house, the gilt chairs in the piano room were covered using offcuts from bridesmaids' dresses made for Mabel's youngest son's wedding, and one of the four-poster beds features the leftovers from a ballgown made during the 1970s.

Sadly, Mabel died before she completed the house, and it is fascinating to contemplate what else she might have had in mind for a house already brimming with carefully crafted miniatures. The dolls' house was bequeathed to the National Trust after her death and given a permanent new home at Overbeck's – a fitting choice, as it sits well alongside the assortment of curiosities amassed by the house's last owner, Otto Overbeck.

Unintentionally, it also echoes the First World War years, when Overbeck's was turned into a convalescent home for wounded soldiers. One of their therapeutic activities was making dolls' house furniture, so Mabel Hill's dolls' house, with its carefully crafted furniture, stands in silent tribute to their memory.

Regency Splendour in Burford

Another replica with strong local links is the dolls' house at the Tolsey Museum in Burford, Oxfordshire. Designed by local architect F. Russell Cox, FRIBA, and built in 1939, the exterior was modelled on Burford's The Great House, a Grade II listed mansion dating from the late seventeenth century.

The interior, designed by Donetta Graham, recreates the opulence of a wealthy family home during the Regency era with its delicately patterned ceilings, elaborately carved fireplaces, gold-panelled walls, elegant wooden furniture and sumptuous soft furnishings. The family are occupied in pursuits typical of the period: the lady of the house stitches her embroidery in the drawing room, a young lady in one of the bedrooms appears to be getting ready to go out while a nurse tends to her baby, and the menfolk in the dining room enjoy a smoke after their meal.

The most interesting aspect of this house, though, is the fact that it throws a spotlight on many of the rural industries that once flourished in this Cotswold town, from weaving, rug-making and basket-making to woodcarving and ironmongery. Every item was handmade by local artists and craftsmen, and a printed guide in the museum lists all the contributors – around seventy in total – with details of the items they made. Local tinsmiths R&J Richards, for example, made the tiny copper kettles in the kitchen, while a local weaver, Miss Murdoch, produced some of the carpets. Artists included watercolour specialist Alban Atkins, a former art master at Burford School, and Helen Bryce, who moved to Burford from Scotland and whose work can also be seen elsewhere in the museum.

Burford's importance in the wool trade is highlighted by the maid sitting at her spinning wheel in the upper gallery, and there are further reminders of the town's industrial past in the richly coloured carpets and coordinating curtains.

Other local connections exist in some of the furniture, which was modelled on items in nearby historic houses. The wardrobe, four-poster bed and entrance ceiling were inspired by those at Chastleton House, an early seventeenth-century house built for wool merchant Walter Jones and now in the care of the National Trust. The sofa, chair and wallpaper in the bedroom were inspired by those at Coleshill

House, a former seventeenth-century country house that was destroyed by fire in 1952.

A music room was added later, again designed by F. Russell Cox and constructed by Frank Earley from the nearby village of Fulbrook. The central attraction is the finely detailed pipe organ, which was made by J. Howard Leech, FRIBA, of Burford and modelled on one by renowned London organ builder Samuel Green. The décor complements that of the main house, with wooden furniture and flooring, portraits on the walls, white busts flanking the organ, and carved panelling.

Recreating Charles Dickens' House in London

Dickens fans might assume that a dolls' house at his former London home would be connected to the man himself. Sadly, this is not the case – but this charming miniature does have its own interesting history. It was built during the 1970s by dolls' house maker Christopher Cole as a model for his book *Make Your Own Dolls' House* (Shepheard-Walwyn, 1976), and is a near-replica of the real house.

No. 48 Doughty Street, the only one of Dickens' former London homes still in existence, is part of a terrace built between 1805 and 1809. The simple but elegant Regency design is typical of the 'spacious and even magnificent houses' (*Morning Chronicle*, 1925) that sprang up in the respectable Bloomsbury area around the turn of the century to accommodate a growing middle-class urban population. Dickens lived here from 1837 to 1839, and in that brief time he completed *The Pickwick Papers*, wrote *Oliver Twist* and

Nicholas Nickleby, and started work on *Barnaby Rudge*. The house and its neighbour, No. 49, were later amalgamated into a lodging house. In 1925 the two properties were opened by the Dickens Fellowship as a museum, and No. 48 has been marked with a blue plaque.

The dolls' house exterior has been closely modelled on No. 48, including the decorative fanlight and arch over the front door, symmetrically arranged windows and simple elevation. The main difference is the roof; Coles chose to replace the rather complicated pitched roof, dormer window and pair of chimney stacks with a simple flat roof. He has also taken the liberty of adding a road sign, 'Doughty St SW1', which doesn't actually appear on the real house! Despite those changes, though, the result is a 1/12 scale model that is unmistakably No. 48 Doughty Street.

The interior, too, has been simplified. The real No. 48 is laid out in typical Regency style: servants' quarters (kitchen, washhouse and scullery) in the basement, entrance hall, dining room and morning room on the ground floor, drawing room and Dickens' study on the first floor, family bedrooms on the second floor and servants' bedroom and the nursery on the top floor.

The dolls' house has retained the same proportions, with storeys of equal height and the rooms on the left-hand side of the house wider than those on the right, which also accommodate the stairs. There are only three levels, and internal doorways have been replaced with partition walls and arches to give easy access to the rooms at the back of the house. The result is a simplification of the layout of No. 48, rather than an exact replica, but it is close enough to give a good impression of the real thing. The dolls' house is currently part of the education team's handling collection, and has been used as a sensory tool for visually impaired visitors to give them an idea of the layout of the house and museum. It is not on public display, but can be viewed by appointment.

A Victorian Fantasy at Grey's Court

If the ghosts of Kitty Carlisle's miniature collection still echo at Grey's Court it's down to Patricia Mackenzie, who was inspired to start building her own dolls' house after visiting the Carlisle Collection during the 1970s when it was still based at this National Trust property.

The Havercroft Mackenzie house quickly became a family project, involving Patricia's mother, husband and children – with various friends also roped in to help – and took forty years to complete. The house resembles a Georgian mansion but the inside is set firmly in the 1860s with a Victorian family and an emphasis on spotlighting some of the inventions of the era.

Like Mabel Hill, Patricia and her family were imaginative in their use of materials. The house itself was constructed from an old sheet of plywood previously used as a window cover after a break-in, and the roof tiles were fashioned from offcuts of their garage felt roofing. The panelled doors were made from old cigar boxes, the posts of the four-poster bed from chopsticks, the blankets in the linen press from outgrown baby vests and the kitchen chair backs from sliced cotton reels.

The grand, sweeping staircase with its decorative balustrades, and the spacious hallway and landing – similar in design to those at Overbeck's – are typically Georgian. The drawing room captures the Georgian 'baroque' style with its painted ceiling, grand central fireplace and Hepplewhite-style couch (made from Elastoplast tins, padded with cotton wool and overlaid with silk).

There is Palladian splendour in the dining room with its ornate blue and cream fireplace (made from a wedding cake pillar cut in half), alcoves (fashioned from baked bean tins) inlaid with statues, the elegant chairs, mahogany table (another cigar box) and plasterwork ceiling with chandelier. The curtains are made from old handkerchiefs.

Much of the rest of the house is typically Victorian, reflecting the Victorians' passion for filling their homes with ornaments, and the dolls are dressed in Victorian fashions. The cosy nursery has toys popular in the Victorian era, including a rocking horse, Noah's Ark, drum, teddy bear and dolls, and at the back of the room is a sewing machine, invented in America in 1845 and available in Britain soon afterwards.

In the bathroom is a flush toilet enclosed in a wooden box, an increasingly popular feature in middle class homes after their appearance at the Great Exhibition in 1851. The toilet roll holder was based on an 1860s model found in the Science Museum in London.

The kitchen shows the gap that still existed in Victorian times between the family and their servants, with a plain wooden table, wooden dresser, copper pots and pans (made from central heating pipes) and tiled floor. A maid scrubs the floor while the cook keeps her eye on the table laden with food.

The lamps, overhead lights and fireplaces throughout the house – even 'below stairs' – are all lit with electricity, another great invention of the Victorian era.

Chapter 7

Dolls' Houses in Literature

'Increasing sentimental interest in children ... produced a mass of literature for and about them ... Stories about dolls' houses are legion.'

Margaret Towner, *The Vivien Greene Dolls'
House Collection* (Cassell, 1995)

Fascination with dolls' houses and all things miniature has inspired many an author to weave a story around a dolls' house, not just for children but for adults too. These go from the whimsical, the ghostly or the macabre to satire and social commentary. The widespread use of dolls' houses in fiction, in a variety of genres, shows the influence they have had over the last 300 years, how they have become part of the nation's consciousness, and how they reflect changing attitudes through the centuries.

Early satire and social commentary
Jonathan Swift (1667–1745) famously explored the idea of smallness in his satirical masterpiece *Gulliver's Travels* (1726), to the extent that Gulliver and Lilliput have become almost synonymous with anything tiny. The land of Lilliput

remains Swift's best-known invention, but in Part II of the book, which sees Gulliver reach the land of Brobdingnag, we have what may be one of the earliest references to a baby house in fiction.

Brobdingnag is the reverse of Lilliput: now Gulliver is the diminutive figure in a land of giants. Kept in captivity by the royal family, who regard him with both fondness and curiosity, Gulliver has a wooden cabinet commissioned for him by the queen to serve as a bedchamber, which contains 'a bed ready furnished by her majesty's upholsterer', as well as 'two chairs, with backs and frames, of a substance not unlike ivory, and two tables, with a cabinet to put my things in'.

When the queen decides she wants Gulliver to dine with her, a miniature table and chair and 'an entire set of silver dishes and plates' are made for him. Gulliver observes that, in comparison to those used by the queen, his 'were not much bigger than what I have seen in a London toy-shop for the furniture of a baby-house'.

In 1879, Norwegian playwright Henrik Ibsen (1828–1906) completed his three-act play *A Doll's House*, which premiered at the Royal Theatre, Copenhagen, on 21 December (the London premiere followed ten years later). Here the dolls' house was used as a metaphor for the way chief protagonist Nora Helmer feels trapped in her male-dominated marriage.

The play inspired a painting of the same name by English artist Sir William Rothenstein (1872–1945), which is now in the Tate collection. The painting won a silver medal at the Paris Exhibition in 1900.

A slightly later example is *The Doll's House* by renowned short story writer Katherine Mansfield (1888–1923). Mansfield was born in New Zealand during its colonial years and through her stories she criticised the rigid social hierarchy that still existed during her childhood and beyond. This theme is central to *The Doll's House*, which was published in 1922 but set in the late 1880s. In an echo of the early baby houses of Europe, this dolls' house is all about power and privilege as well as popularity, acceptance and rejection.

The wealthy Burnell sisters, Isabel, Lottie and Kezia, are given a dolls' house, and despite the rather strong smell of paint it is declared a 'perfect, perfect little house'. The 'dark, oily, spinach green' house has a front that swings right open, much to the children's joy. For them the house is 'too marvellous … they had never seen anything like it in their lives'.

Already popular at school, the Burnell sisters become even more popular when their friends find out about the dolls' house. On their way to school, the sisters look forward to boasting about the house and argue about which of them should be the first to tell everyone. Inevitably that privilege falls to Isabel, the eldest. Excitingly, their mother has said they can bring their friends home to see the house, two at a time, giving the Burnell sisters an extra feeling of power and importance.

The only girls not included in this invitation are the Kelvey sisters, Lil and Else, who are deemed unfit for most of the pupils at the school to mix with. Rather like the dolls in the Burnells' dolls' house, which 'were really too big' for the house and 'didn't look as though they belonged', the Kelvey girls don't belong socially. When Kezia Burnell relents and brings the Kelveys home to see the dolls' house, her mother is furious and orders the Kelvey girls to leave. Like most of Katherine Mansfield's stories, this one pulls no punches.

Stories for children

One of the earliest and most famous children's stories centred around a dolls' house is *The Tale of Two Bad Mice*, the fifth of the little books by Beatrix Potter (1866–1943), published by Frederick Warne & Sons in 1904.

The dolls' house at Hill Top, Beatrix Potter's former Lake District home (now owned by the National Trust), is not the one that featured in the book, as sometimes thought: that honour goes to a dolls' house made by her publisher, Norman Warne, for his niece, Winifred. When Beatrix saw the nearly completed dolls' house in Warne's basement she knew she had found the perfect setting for her new story about two naughty mice.

Beatrix never got to see the finished dolls' house, so she worked from photographs and drawings while writing the book. But Warne was able to borrow some dolls from his nieces, as well as providing her with a range of dolls' house food and kitchen equipment from Hamley's, and from these Beatrix began to write about a 'very beautiful doll's-house' that belonged to two dolls, Lucinda and Jane.

Alas for Lucinda and Jane, while they are out one morning their lovely home is ransacked and vandalised by the two bad mice, Tom Thumb and Hunca Munca, who angrily smash the food when they discover it isn't real but find lots of other delights to steal for their own home – a bolster from Lucinda's bed, some clothes, a chair, a cradle, and pots and pans. Afterwards, ashamed of what they have done, they put a crooked sixpence in the doll's stocking on Christmas Eve and Hunca Munca goes every morning to sweep the dolls' house with her broom.

Beatrix dedicated the book to Winifred: 'For W.M.L.W., the little girl who had the dolls' house'.

The dolls' house on display at Hill Top was bought by Beatrix much later and is believed to date from around 1865. It is now home to many of the objects featured in *The Tale of Two Bad Mice*, including the dolls' house food that Tom Thumb and Hunca Munca tried to eat, the cutlery, kitchen equipment, bellows, coal scuttle and other items that Norman bought for Beatrix from Hamley's. Also in Beatrix's bedroom are the French dolls believed to have been the models for Jane and Lucinda.

Winifred Warne's original dolls' house, the model for *The Tale of Two Bad Mice*, appears to have been lost.

A complete contrast is the 1947 children's novel *The Dolls' House* by Rumer Godden (1907-1998). Unlike Potter's charming, feel-good tale, this one draws on the emotions with its exploration of both kindness and cruel, abusive behaviour. The story revolves around Tottie Plantaganet, a 100-year-old Dutch wooden doll who lives with her parents, little brother Apple and Darner the dog in two cramped, draughty shoeboxes. The dolls dream of having a proper house to live in, and their owners, Emily and Charlotte, try to find something suitable. Then a Victorian dolls' house, which once belonged to Emily and Charlotte's great-grandmother and Great-Great-Aunt Laura, is discovered in an attic, and finally Tottie and her family have somewhere nice to live. The only problem is that the house comes with the beautiful but vain, selfish china doll Marchpane, who causes havoc in the little house, leading ultimately to tragedy.

The book was made into a television series, *Tottie: The Story of a Doll's House*, by Smallfilms in 1984.

Stories written for Queen Mary

Among the 200 books written for the library in Queen Mary's dolls' house (see Chapter 5), two are stories about dolls' houses. M.R. James (1862–1936) wrote *The Haunted Dolls' House* in 1922, and it was subsequently published in *The Empire Review* (1923) and the anthology *A Warning to the Curious and Other Ghost Stories* (1925). James was one of the best-known ghost story writers of the late nineteenth and early twentieth centuries, and his stories were notable for their realistic settings while often being inspired by his interest in antiquities.

In *The Haunted Dolls' House*, antiques dealer Dillet manages to acquire an antique dolls' house at a bargain price, and when he first gets it home he admires its exquisite furnishings. But that night, he is woken up by a clock striking one o'clock and suddenly he can see inside the dolls' house even though it is dark. To his horror, he witnesses the grandfather doll being murdered by poisoning. Later, 'a new sort of light ... a pale ugly light' creeps around the door of the two children's bedroom, a strange creature enters and Dillet can hear the 'sound of cries ... infinitely appalling'. A 'hideous commotion' all over the dolls' house follows, and shortly afterwards Dillet sees two small coffins being carried out of the house.

The next day, Dillet visits a museum and finds the burial records of a family called Merewether, whose lives seem to mirror those of the dolls in the dolls' house. Unable to get rid of the dolls' house, he puts it in the loft and covers it with a sheet.

A rather more cheerful tale was written by Vita Sackville-West for the dolls' house library. *A Note of Explanation*, created in miniature in 1924, was published for the first time in 2017 in a cloth-bound book with colourful illustrations by Kate Baylay and an afterword by Sackville-West's biographer, Matthew Dennison.

This charming and witty story is all about a sprite who moves into Queen Mary's dolls' house, 'a dolls' house so marvellously made that from far and near people come to look at it', and makes herself at home, sleeping in a different bedroom each night, trying out all the 'great many things she had never seen before' and causing chaos along the way.

Sackville-West's sprite is said to have influenced the creation of Virginia Woolf's time-travelling poet Orlando, and her 1928 novel was dedicated to Sackville-West.

From the whimsical to the macabre

Stories and novels about dolls' house, for both children and adults, have become hugely varied from the mid-twentieth century onwards. Most children's fiction preserves the ideal of the lovely, charming and sometimes magical image of a dolls' house, but in adult fiction dolls' houses are often seen as menacing, sinister, diabolical – things to be feared rather than admired. It's a long way from the eighteenth-century vision of a perfect miniature world.

Jessie Burton (b. 1982) tapped into this with *The Miniaturist* (2014), in which a Dutch cabinet house becomes threatening and creepy, while also – like Ibsen's *The Dolls' House* – becoming a metaphor for the claustrophobic life of a woman in a male-dominated world.

The story was inspired by Petronella Oortman's cabinet house (see Chapter 1) after the author saw it on display at the Rijksmuseum in Amsterdam. Now an international bestseller, the novel whisks the reader into the affluent society of seventeenth-century Amsterdam, at the heart of which is the sumptuous cabinet house given to new bride Nella by her wealthy merchant husband Johannes Brandt.

For Burton, the Oortman house highlighted 'the restrictive, elusive nature of a woman's domestic sphere' (*The Independent*, 10 December 2014), and Nella instantly finds the house disconcerting: the tiny rooms are 'dead ends', and the 'exposed interior ... begins to make her uneasy', as if she is being watched. Unlike most rich society women, she has no family or friends to come and admire the house, and it seems to her to be 'a monument to her powerlessness'.

Nella's sense of unease continues as a mysterious miniaturist helps furnish the cabinet house, sending unasked-for miniatures that seem to be mocking her and predicting her future. The house becomes a symbol of Nella's loveless marriage and the fact that she feels constrained and alienated by her elusive husband and hostile sister-in-law.

Burton's novel has won several awards, and was filmed by the BBC for a three-part television adaptation in 2017.

Phoebe Morgan's *The Doll House* (2018) is similarly creepy, with the heroine, Corinne, feeling threatened as pieces from her childhood dolls' house mysteriously turn up at her flat, one by one. Someone knows too much about her life, and they are seeking revenge.

Children's books tend to keep the dolls' house dream alive, with stories such as Robyn Johnson's *The Enchanted Dolls' House* (2005) and Jane Ray's *The Dolls' House Fairy* (2010).

As dolls' houses continue to be popular, among both children and adults, no doubt they will continue to inspire novelists and short story writers.

Chapter 8

Miniatures Move Outside:
Model Towns and Villages

'...boys' play on a smashing adult scale, defying all common sense but glorious in its absorption in the exquisitely useless'.

> J.B. Priestley, *English Journey*
> (Heinemann & Gollancz, 1934),
> on Wolf's Cove, Snowshill

With dolls' houses enjoying unprecedented popularity by the end of the nineteenth century, it was perhaps inevitable that miniatures would start to venture outside. The fascination with miniature versions of towns, villages and railways from the early twentieth century was a natural progression from dolls' houses, with the same potential for allowing the imagination to take flight. From focusing on a single dolls' house, people could now walk along whole streets of miniatures, Gulliver-like, admiring their Lilliputian charm. Model villages were quirky and different, and opened up an exciting new world at a time when people were looking for a bit of escapism. And, unlike dolls' houses, which were largely the preserve of women and girls, model villages were something that anyone could enjoy.

The growing interest in model railways and miniature landscapes from the early twentieth century was another contributory factor, and many of the early model villages evolved around miniature railways.

The fact that many model towns and villages replicate real places, or capture typical scenes from a specific era, has become an added bonus with the passing of time: like dolls' houses, these miniatures are now slices of social history.

Bekonscot Model Railway and Village

The granddaddy of them all, Bekonscot was the one that set the trend for model villages in Britain when it first opened its doors to the public on 4 August 1929. It was not quite the first, as is often believed – Charles Paget Wade's Fladbury had sprung into life in Hampstead in 1908, later to be moved to Snowshill and given a new identity as Wolf's Cove (see Chapter 10) – but Bekonscot is the oldest model village in continuous existence and has outlasted many of its twentieth-century rivals. Time has stood still at Bekonscot, as it is firmly rooted in the 1930s, reflecting the architecture, fashions and lifestyle of the day.

It all started when London accountant Roland Callingham (1879–1961) was given an ultimatum by his wife – either his model railway left, or she would. And so emerged the beginnings of what would become one of the most famous model villages in the world. Callingham commissioned model-railway experts Basset-Lowke to lay out a Gauge 1 model railway, ably assisted by his friend James Shilcock. Soon after, Callingham and his gardener, Tom Berry, gave the garden pond a pier and some islands, and built a few model houses. The model village was starting to take shape.

One of the earliest buildings was the church, built by Berry in the Early English style with stained glass windows by artist Edmund Dulac. Timbered houses, thatched cottages, shops and other buildings began to sprawl along the tiny roads. Six separate villages and hamlets were eventually established, each with its own distinctive character, from the Evenlode town and mining village to the seaside town of Splashyng. Since then, the village has continued to evolve, and new buildings are still being added.

Its opening in 1929 brought instant fame. Headlines flashed across the world, bringing thousands of visitors through the gates – including, in 1934, Queen Mary with her two young granddaughters, Princesses Elizabeth and Margaret Rose, the day before Princess Elizabeth's eighth birthday. It was the first of several royal visits over the years.

The name Bekonscot was coined in 1932, and was an amalgamation of Beaconsfield – using the old spelling of 'Bekon' – and Callingham's former home town of Ascot. The same year, modest charges were introduced, with any profits at the end of the year going to charity – a practise that continues to this day. An old brochure from the 1930s shows that the admission charge was 1 shilling for adults and 6d for children, with proceeds destined for the Railway Benevolent Institution and the Queen's Institute of District Nursing.

Most of the buildings are imaginary, but one exception is Marks & Spencer, which was based on the M&S in High Wycombe as it was in the 1930s and is the smallest M&S in the world. Beaconsfield Station has also been recreated.

Another exact replica is Green Hedges, the former Beaconsfield home of Enid Blyton (1897–1968). The renowned children's author moved to Green Hedges in 1938 and lived there until shortly before her death in 1968, and it was here that she wrote most of her books. A regular visitor to the model village, she became a friend of Callingham's and was inspired to write the short story *The Enchanted Village* in 1953. Her real home was later demolished but lives on through the model version, which was added to Bekonscot in 1997 to mark the centenary of her birth. The author can be seen sitting on a garden bench typing, while Noddy's car is parked in the driveway.

In 2009, Bekonscot was the setting for the *Midsomer Murders* episode 'Small Mercies', in which the first unfortunate victim was found pegged down like Gulliver, his brutal death at odds with the idyllic English pastoral scenes portrayed by the model village.

Bekonscot has recently celebrated its 90th birthday, and this particular birthday boy is still young at heart, with a spring in his step and with an eye very much on the future. In 2000, a time capsule was buried beneath a replica of the Bucks Free Press office in High Wycombe as it was in the 1930s. This time capsule is set to be unearthed for Bekonscot's centenary in 2029. Meanwhile, visitors are still streaming through in vast numbers, and Roland

Callingham's trains continue to snake merrily around the model village, the delight that they generate undimmed by the passage of time.

Bourton-on-the-Water Model Village

This one-ninth scale replica of the famous Gloucestershire village – known as the Little Venice of the Cotswolds – is the only model village in the country to have been awarded Grade II listed status by English Heritage in recognition of its historical importance, attention to detail and authenticity. It was also the first to be established specifically as a visitor attraction – inspired, no doubt, by the success of Bekonscot.

Established in the back garden of the eighteenth-century Old New Inn in the 1930s, the model village was the brainchild of former landlord C.A. Morris who, together with his wife, painstakingly measured the real village, from the inn to the eighteenth-century water mill (now home to the Cotswold Motoring Museum), to ensure pinpoint accuracy. With the help of eight local builders, and using stone from two local quarries, he then set about recreating the village in miniature. Building began in 1936, and the village officially opened to the public in May 1937 to celebrate the Coronation of King George VI and Queen Elizabeth. It was another three years before the village was finally completed.

As you enter the model village, it really is like stepping back in time as you gaze on the microcosm of 1930s Cotswold life spread before you. Unlike most model villages, though, which capture and preserve a specific era, this one moves with the times. As buildings in the real village change their model versions are updated, so they are always a true reflection of the real Bourton-on-the-Water. Happily, there have been remarkably few significant changes over the last eighty years, so even with a few modern shop fronts the village still has a distinctly 1930s feel to it.

A replica River Windrush flows through the centre of the village, spanned by the famous stone bridges, with the miniature trees lining its banks mirrored in the water. Notable landmarks include the Cotswold Motoring Museum, the Cotswold Birdland Park and Gardens (complete with some delightful miniature penguins) and the impressive war memorial.

Bourton-on-the-Water has two churches and both are reproduced here in loving detail, from the elegant St Lawrence Church with its eye-catching Georgian tower to the late nineteenth century Baptist Church. Both churches have the sound of choirs within.

A famous inclusion is the model of the model village, which in turn contains a model of the model, which also contains a model, and so on, like a set of Russian dolls.

Perhaps most delightful of all are the quaint Cotswold houses and shops bordering the streets, each with its own unique character and with the tiniest details meticulously recreated. The miniature shrubberies and trees are equally enchanting, and many have survived from when the village was first planted. A mixture of deciduous and evergreen trees, including alpines and conifers, gives a realistic effect, and these are kept to scale by regular pruning. Real turf is used for the lawns, and again is cut regularly.

Since 2004, the model village has also been home to the Exhibition of Miniatures, a collection of around thirty miniature scenes, shops and room settings that previously existed as Miniature World in Bourton's High Street. Among this collection are elegant drawing rooms from the Georgian and Victorian eras, a packed fruit and vegetable stall, a flower shop, a 1920s fashion house and a nature study day at a local school. The largest and most evocative scene is a 1940s dock basin featuring a railway, barges, wharf-side buildings and an assortment of people, all combining to give an impression of bustling activity.

There is humour too, in the gardener enjoying a quiet moment in his shed, the wife with her lover looking somewhat startled as the husband makes an unexpectedly early return, and a family of mice in a cosy, wooden-beamed cottage.

The collection was created by more than a hundred of England's leading miniaturists.

Another addition to the model village is the Miniature Landscape Exhibition, which opened in 2014. This set of seven cottages was the work of Somerset craftsman John Constable, author of *Landscapes in Miniature* (Lutterworth Press, 1984) and *Understanding Cottages* (Capall Bann Publishing, 2002).

The result of years of research, these 1/32-scale cottages are made from traditional materials and between them contain thousands of individually crafted bricks, rafters, windows and doors, all created with tools Constable made himself. The cottages took twenty-five years to complete, and each is displayed in its own landscaped setting inspired by Constable's own books.

The collection is now an important historical record of traditional rural cottages representing a bygone age. Some are based on actual buildings, such as Teapot Hall in Scrivelsby, Lincolnshire, which was sadly demolished in the 1940s, and Willy Lott's Cottage in East Bergholt, Suffolk, which featured in *The Hay Wain* by the English Romantic painter John Constable. There's also Thomas Hardy's cottage in Higher Brockhampton, Dorset, as it looked in Hardy's day; it was here that he wrote *Under the Greenwood Tree* and *Far from the Madding Crowd*. Other cottages are recreations of styles typical of a specific era, such as the medieval Wealden house found in the Weald of Kent, and a medieval cruck cottage.

Wimborne Model Town

Like Bourton-on-the-Water, the model town at Wimborne is a recreation of the town in which it sits. Unlike Bourton, though, time has stood still at Wimborne; it captures the town exactly as it was in the 1950s, offering a fascinating glimpse into Wimborne's past.

Conceived during the late 1940s by local businessman Charles Coffen, following a visit to the model village at Bourton, the 1/10-scale model opened its doors to visitors in 1951. Built from concrete panels with beech window frames, the buildings were exact replicas of those in the town, with shops displaying goods typical of the era. It quickly became a popular tourist attraction, with visitors coming from all over the UK.

By the 1980s, the model town had fallen into disrepair and it closed in 1983. Its original site near the Cornmarket, north-west of the famous minster, was purchased by a property developer and the model seemed doomed for demolition. It was reprieved when local landowner Sir Michael Hanham (1922–2009) offered use of the current site south of King Street.

Moving the models from the old site to the new one was a long, painstaking process, but in 1991 the miniature town was officially reopened by Roy Castle, just six months before he was tragically diagnosed with cancer. Soon visitors were once again swarming through the streets of the model town, and it has continued to attract thousands of visitors annually ever since.

In addition to the annual maintenance of the shop fronts, which can become damaged during the summer season, retaining the 1950s appearance with as much historical accuracy as possible is considered essential. As you stroll through its streets, there is a poignant reminder of the days before towns became dominated by high street chains. Here you will find all those shops that are rapidly disappearing from our towns and cities: a hardware store, sweet shop, butcher, ironmonger, fishmonger and bakery, as well as typically English tea rooms, quaint old pubs and hotels, old-fashioned ladies' and gents' hairdressers and many more, all conjuring up an era that has long gone. There is even a

Woolworth's store; in the real town, this building was long ago taken over by Fat Face.

Inside the shops, you can see miniature wares on sale, some purchased from dolls' house shops and others made in the model town's own workshops. One shop features a range of books, for example, created by photocopying the covers of a real book, reducing them to scale and sticking them on blocks of wood.

As is often the case with model villages, there is a bit of quirky humour here too. If you listen carefully at the public telephone box at the end of East Street you can hear the phone ringing, while at the public toilets in Park Lane you can hear the sound of toilets flushing!

The crowning glory is the recreation of Wimborne Minster, where a wedding is taking place and there is music playing. A group of Brownies can be seen providing the guard of honour, in recognition of the local Brownies who collected money for the model town in its early years.

If you look westwards, you can see the towers of the real Wimborne Minster, the town's most famous landmark, peeping through the trees. One of its best-known features is its clock, the Quarter Jack, on the north face of the west tower. This was originally the figure of a monk, crafted in 1612, but changed to that of a Grenadier during the Napoleonic wars. The real Quarter Jack strikes every quarter of an hour, and the miniature replica strikes just after it.

Since 2014, Wimborne Model Town has also been home to the Beryl Dade Dolls' House Collection. This was donated by local resident Beryl Dade, who had collected and refurbished the houses over a period of fifteen years. When the collection of more than twenty dolls' houses had taken over several rooms in her house, she presented fifteen of them to the model town.

The 1/12 scale miniatures are all illuminated, and for each one Beryl has invented a fun, light-hearted story featuring a cast of interesting, quirky and eccentric characters. There are also various shops and cafes, as well as a restaurant bearing the delightful name 'Mr T.R. Eats'.

The only house based on real life is Rose Villa, a recreation of Beryl's childhood home in Chalford, South East London, where she grew up during the Second World War.

Other more unusual items in the collection include a gypsy caravan, a fairy house and a teddy bear's house.

Corfe Castle Model Village

Built to a scale of 1/20, Corfe Castle Model Village is smaller than most, a bijou creation that enables you to see the whole of Corfe Castle village spread out in miniature before you. The brainchild of local newsagent Eddie Holland, the model village recreates the real village as it looked in the mid-seventeenth century: a tiny community nestled in the shadow of its mighty castle, which was built by William the Conqueror and later became home to Royalist supporters Sir John and Lady Mary Bankes before Roundhead soldiers destroyed it on Cromwell's orders.

Eddie Holland commissioned another local man, Jack Phillips, to create the models, and the village opened two years later, on 7 April 1966. Phillips had faithfully recreated the village houses, shops and other buildings to the tiniest detail, constructing the models from wooden frames and overlaying them with concrete. Most of the roofs were made from local Purbeck stone, with the tiles individually hand crafted.

The Potting Shed, where Phillips carried out all this work, is now a small museum telling the story of Corfe Castle Model Village as well as giving a general history of model villages. A picture of Eddie Holland and his wife, Edna, inspecting the model village in 1965 shows how little it has changed in the last fifty-five years.

As in the real village, the focal point is the castle, where cattle can be seen grazing by the moat while a group of women cook over a roaring fire. Above the outer gatehouse, a member of the Royalist army keeps watch over the village, cannons and other artillery at the ready. As you gaze at the miniature castle in all its original glory, you can see the ruins of the real one forming a rather forlorn, skeletal backdrop.

Nearby is a replica of Boar Mill, an eighteenth-century corn mill that was still working until the mid-twentieth century and is now owned by the National Trust. Among the shops lining the streets is E.O. Holland, a recreation of the shop that Eddie Holland once owned in the village centre. Other buildings of interest include the eighteenth-century Town House, with its distinctive bow window, the Museum and Town Hall (formerly a prison), Morton House Hotel (originally an Elizabethan manor) and the Fox Inn, reputedly the oldest pub in England.

A wedding party has gathered at St Edward's Parish Church, which dates back to the thirteenth century, although much of it was rebuilt in 1860. The choir can be heard in the church, and if you peer closely at the tower, a survival from the fifteenth century, you can see mice climbing towards the clock!

One of the features of this village is the miniature figures dotted around the place, engaged in a variety of everyday activities – and sometimes raising questions in the viewer's mind, such as the rather forlorn figure huddled up on a bench near the church. The figures were commissioned by previous owners Ed and Emily Paris, who ran the model village from 2002–2017. Just outside the model village is a stone bench dedicated to the memory of its first owner, Eddie Holland, the man responsible for this miniature haven.

More to explore

Inevitably, not all of the model villages that sprang up during the 20th century have survived, but there are still many dotted around the country.

The original displays at Pendon Museum in Oxfordshire were created in 1954 by Australian model-maker Roye England (1908-1995), who wanted to preserve, in miniature, a fragment of rural England that was fast disappearing. The centrepiece of the museum is a recreation of the Vale of White Horse as it looked in the 1930s, complete with miniature trains, hills, fields, farms and thatched cottages. In addition, there is the Dartmoor scene, featuring Brunel's timber viaduct, and the Madder Valley model railway, built by modelling pioneer John Ahern during the 1930s and donated to Pendon on his death in 1961.

A slightly later model village is the one at Babbacombe, in Devon, which was opened by Tom Dobbins in 1963 and now has more than 400 buildings and a model railway set in four acres of gardens, representing English life over six decades. The model village is constantly evolving, with new models and other attractions being added every year. Babbacombe has popped up in several BBC television programmes, including *The Graham Norton Show*, *The One Show* and *Don't Forget the Driver*.

A recent addition to the miniature scene is the model railway at Bexhill Museum in East Sussex. A childhood toy of comedian Eddie Izzard and his brother, Mark, the model was started by their father, Harold John Izzard, in 1959 and donated to Bexhill Museum by the family in 2016. It has since been extended by members of the Bexhill Model Railway Club to reflect Sidley and Bexhill in the 1940s, with scale models of buildings and landmarks connected to the Izzard family. Eddie Izzard – a patron of the museum since 2007 – dedicated the railway in memory of his father on 28 September 2018, and officially opened the completed layout on 16 September 2019.

Chapter 9

Collecting Dolls' Houses

'Collecting is not acquiring. It is more like planning a delightful small party, where everyone will find a friend and feel at home. Collecting should be thought of as tenderly as gardening.'

Vivien Greene, *The Vivien Greene Dolls' House Collection* (Cassell, 1995)

In May 2017, an early Georgian dolls' house sold at Sotheby's for an eye-watering £78,000 (including VAT). The rare wooden baby house, dating from 1720–30, was due to be exported by the buyer when the government stepped in and put a temporary halt to proceedings on the grounds that the house was of cultural importance to the nation. Believed to be one of only around thirty baby houses surviving from the early eighteenth century, the house had been in the Forster family for around 250 years, including at one time being in the ownership of Liberal MP William Edward Forster (1818–1886). Having saved the baby house from disappearing from UK shores, the search was on for a new buyer. Eventually it was purchased by the V&A Museum of Childhood, where it is currently in storage.

Just months before the Sotheby's sale, an even more staggering price was paid for an early eighteenth-century Dutch cabinet house at the European Fine Art Foundation (TEFAF) Fair in Maastricht, Netherlands. The exquisite nine-room cabinet, filled with miniature porcelain dishes and silver tankards, and featuring two drawers and elaborate base, was snapped up early on the first day for a cool $1.8 million.

Fortunately, you don't have to be able to lay your hands on this kind of money to become a dolls' house collector. Asking prices do vary, though, so depending on what you're after you could pay anything from a fiver to several thousand pounds. You can expect to pay more at auction houses, where you are more likely to find rare and valuable items, so if you're after something a little more modest, then antique shops and eBay are better options and you can sometimes bag some fantastic bargains.

Getting started

You probably already have a good idea of the kind of dolls' house you want, but if you're not sure then it's worth strolling around some antique shops, dolls' house shops and dolls' house fairs to see what's available and what appeals to you. Joining a dolls' house club can be helpful too, if you have one in your area. Any of these options give you the opportunity to chat to experts and fellow enthusiasts, who are usually happy to help.

There are also some good online specialists, such as the Dolls House Emporium and Maple Street Dolls Houses and Miniatures, both of which sell a wide range of dolls' houses, furniture, lighting, accessories and figures from a variety of different brands.

Another store worth a look is The Dolls House at Northleach, near Cheltenham. Established in London in 1971 by Michal Morse, and relocated to Northleach in 1995, this was the first specialist dolls' house shop in England. Its stocks include a wide range of antique and second-hand dolls' houses, including well-known brands such as Triang, as well as dolls, furniture and accessories.

Before you buy anything, don't forget to consider the space you have available, and whether a particular style will look right in your home. Something that looks very appealing nestling snugly among other vintage items in an antiques shop might look completely out of place when you get it home. Also, it's easy to get carried away with enthusiasm if you see something you like, but do check its condition carefully. If it's a bit battered and some of the paint is missing, are you able to restore it? Is it in need of major repair? Some older houses can have dry rot or woodworm, in which case they are best avoided no matter how charming they look!

For some people, of course, restoring a dolls' house is what the hobby is all about, and if that's what you're looking for then you can probably snap up some good bargains. If you prefer to buy something that needs minimal attention, so that you can focus on making and buying lovely furnishings for it, then you need to be a bit fussier!

It's worth making sure you know what kind of project you're after before you dive in. Do you want to decorate your dolls' house in the style of a specific era, or do you prefer a mix of styles? Do you know which scale you prefer? The most common scale is 1/12, which is a good size if you don't want something that's too small and fiddly. If you don't have much space and need something a bit smaller, 1/24 is also a nice size. It's best to try to stick to one scale throughout so that everything is in proportion, but you can occasionally get away with sneaking in the odd item that strays from the rules!

Antique and vintage dolls' houses

Anyone with an interest in the historical aspect of dolls' houses may well be tempted to look for antique or vintage houses.

Antique houses – generally defined as those over 100 years old – obviously tend to be both expensive and difficult to track down. Georgian houses rarely come up, but dolls' houses from the late nineteenth and early twentieth centuries are a little more plentiful and don't necessarily cost the earth. Over the last few years, auction houses such as Sotheby's and Bonhams have sold mid- to late nineteenth-century houses for as little as £150 right up to several thousand pounds. An English painted wooden dolls' house and contents, for example, dating from c.1848, sold in 2015 for £9,375.

Vintage dolls' houses, loosely defined as those less than 100 but more than 50 years old, are naturally more plentiful but can also vary hugely in price, depending on their availability, condition, size and whether they are furnished or not. The mass-produced dolls' houses of the first half of the twentieth century, such as Lines Brothers/Triang, mostly fall into this category. A recent eBay search brought up a Triang thatched cottage for £500, Triang Stockbrokers house for £450 and Triang St Claire's Hospital from the 1930s for £325. However, there were also smaller Triang houses for as little as £30. You can also stock up on dolls' house furniture and accessories from eBay for as little as £5. Whether you are after a complete dolls' house or additional items for an existing house, there is plenty of choice.

The Dolls House in Northleach had similar variations during a recent search, with some Triang models on sale for less than £100, but with others considerably more expensive – such as the No.93, in original condition with fireplaces and kitchen/bathroom fittings, which was priced at £450. Some earlier Lines models cost several hundred pounds, with a 1909 model priced at £550.

Other brands fetch similar prices. A Hobbies Tudor-style house was priced at £300 on eBay recently, and there were several Lundby models with prices varying from £300 to £800.

Dolls' house furniture and accessories are a similar story, with prices ranging from less than £100 to several hundred for rarer items in good condition.

Modern

Dolls' houses from the mid-twentieth century onwards generally tend to be much more affordable, although they are more likely to have been heavily played with so can be in need of some refurbishment. These houses are great for a trip down memory lane to your own childhood days, but you might need to spend some time and money getting them back to good condition, so that's something to factor in on top of the cost of the house itself.

If that's not for you, then consider buying (or commissioning, if you can afford it!) a brand new house. These come in a huge range of styles, from Tudor, Georgian or Victorian, to something more reflective of the twentieth or twenty-first centuries.

You then need to decide whether you want a fully furnished house, which will cost a bit more, or whether you want an unfurnished house that will cost less and give you the pleasure of choosing the contents yourself. The latter certainly has a lot more potential for a fun, fulfilling hobby as you gradually build up a range of furniture, soft furnishings and accessories to give your dolls' house a unique identity.

Dolls' house kits have become increasingly popular, and these can be a satisfying challenge as well as a bit cheaper than buying a ready-made house. If you don't have much space, shops and room settings are another option, perhaps based on a theme or set in a specific era. Any of these are easily obtainable from places like Maple Street, Hobbies or the Dolls House Emporium. For shops and room settings, the Carlisle Collection in Chapter 6 might give you a few ideas!

The possibilities are endless, and there really is something to suit all tastes and wallets these days. The variety of options and the challenge of creating something unique is all part of the pleasure of the dolls' house hobby.

Chapter 10

Some Notable Collectors

'The love of extremely miniature work is probably an aspect of some obscure mental disease, but it's great fun nevertheless.'

Patrick Murray, founder and first curator
of Museum of Childhood, Edinburgh

There have been many notable collectors since dolls' houses became a universally accessible hobby during the twentieth century, and some have made a significant contribution to our understanding and appreciation of dolls' houses and other miniatures. Below are just a few who have left an important legacy to the dolls' house world.

Betty Cadbury

If Betty Cadbury's name instantly conjures up thoughts of chocolate it's not surprising – she did, after all, marry into the famous manufacturing company. But her life was devoted to collecting and studying equally tempting but much longer-lasting sweet treats – dolls, dolls' houses and almost every other toy imaginable. She became an authority on the subject, writing articles for the Antique

Collectors' Club and Doll Club of Washington, researching for television and film companies and undertaking lecture tours in the UK and overseas.

Betty was born on 21 September 1915 to Leslie and Ella Hone and spent her childhood in Winchester, where her grandfather was head of the cathedral choir school. The collecting habit came later on; her early working life, during the Second World War, was in nursing, secretarial and voluntary museum work.

During the war she met Christopher Cadbury (1908–1995), and the couple married in 1958. They settled in Beaconswood, Rednal, near Birmingham, where Betty became active in local affairs, serving as a Labour councillor and as governor of two primary schools. Meanwhile, her husband, a wildlife conservationist, was appointed President of the Royal Society for Nature Conservancy in 1962, a post he held for twenty-six years.

It was during the 1960s, when she was well into her 40s, that Betty found her true vocation. A chance discovery of a wax doll in a local junk shop sparked an interest in collecting and studying toys, and what started as a hobby eventually turned into a full-time career. Her focus was not on collecting expensive items for display purposes, but on delving into the lives of the people who made and played with the toys. Her firm belief was that every toy had its own story to tell.

As her collection grew, she established the Museum of Playthings Past at her Birmingham home, displaying all kinds of toys from dolls and dolls' houses to pull-along toys, tinplate toys, paper toys, indoor and outdoor games and much more. She was particularly fascinated by mechanical toys, which she took great delight in demonstrating to museum visitors.

In 1976 her collection was the basis for her book *Playthings Past* (David & Charles, 1976), which gives an overview of a broad range of toys from the seventeenth to mid-twentieth centuries, along with detailed insights into their manufacture, social history and collectability. The book helped cement Betty's reputation as a toy specialist, and she was frequently invited to give talks and to appear on television programmes.

Her endeavours were fully supported by her husband, and in *Playthings Past* she includes an acknowledgement to 'my husband Christopher, with love and thanks for the shared enthusiasm'.

Betty died on 11 April 1991, aged 75, but her collection lives on, now owned by the Betty Cadbury Trust and cared for by the National Trust at the Museum of Childhood within Sudbury Hall. Among the many items on display are several furnished dolls' houses and dolls.

A highlight is the 1890 model that features in Betty's *Playthings Past*. This house is typical of the large, spacious houses occupied by a wealthy family and their servants during the late Victorian era. It has an imposing grey frontage (which has been removed and displayed behind the house to expose the interior), with pale green sides and a darker green roof with two dormers, two chimney stacks and a central pediment featuring five stars mounted on discs. The front door portico has carved pillars on plinths with a small pediment featuring a heart within a carved circle. Unusually for a dolls' house, it has rooms both front and back – thirteen in all – connected by sixteen internal doors. The furnishings include both commercial and handmade items from the late nineteenth century up to the 1940s.

There is also a model schoolroom dating from around 1900, which was made in France and has wooden desks, a large floor-standing abacus, educational posters on the walls and bisque dolls. More dolls of all sizes are in separate display cases, and include Grodnertal dolls from around 1825, miniature Dutch dolls and bisque 'Frozen Charlotte' dolls from the mid-nineteenth century and a Japanese doll from the early twentieth century.

The collection at Sudbury Hall includes many more items not on display, notably some of Betty's letters and ring binders containing her notes about the collection. For each item, she carefully recorded the date purchased, price paid and seller's name and address, as well as a description and sometimes a photograph.

There are, of course, other dolls' houses, miniatures and toys on display that complement the Betty Cadbury collection, resulting in a permanent, hugely varied exhibition that brings the story of children and their playthings right up to the twenty-first century.

Vivien Greene

Vivien Greene's collection of around fifty English dolls' houses, spanning the Georgian, Victorian and Edwardian eras, established her as one of the leading dolls' house specialists of the twentieth century.

Born Vivienne Dayrell-Browning in 1905, she began collecting dolls and dolls' house furniture as a child. An unsettled, peripatetic childhood – culminating in her parents separating when she was 15 – made her long for a permanent home and planted the seeds of her interest in houses and furnishings.

She married novelist Graham Greene in 1927 at St Mary's Church, Hampstead Heath, and they had two children – Lucy (b. 1933) and Francis (b. 1936).

Vivien and the girls were evacuated to Oxford during the Second World War, living first in the city centre and later moving to Grove House at Iffley, on the outskirts of the city. When a bomb destroyed their London home, Vivien began trawling local auctions to replace lost possessions, accompanied by Oxford historian A.J.P. Taylor.

A chance sighting of an antique dolls' house at an auction in Burford in 1944 was the catalyst for a major new hobby that sustained her during the rest of the war and became a welcome distraction from her husband's infidelities and their eventual separation in 1948. She continued to collect dolls' houses after the war, cleaning and restoring them, researching their history and filling them with authentic furnishings.

In *The Vivien Greene Dolls' House Collection* (Cassell, 1995) she wrote that both home and dolls' house collection gave her 'immense pleasure ... I have most happily been able to combine having a loved permanent home and indulging, in miniature, my enjoyment of all kinds and periods of English domestic architecture and decoration'.

Eventually she travelled all over the UK and overseas, adding to her own dolls' house collection and recording details of as many others as possible for posterity. She filled numerous notebooks with drawings and descriptions of more than 1500 dolls' houses, including Ann Sharp's house (see Chapter 2) and the dolls' house at Uppark (see Chapter 3).

Out of this came her first book, *English Dolls' Houses of the Eighteenth and Nineteenth Centuries* (Batsford, 1955), which established dolls' houses as important pieces of social history and Vivien as the leading authority of the day. The book attracted widespread interest, prompting Vivien to display her collection in a purpose-built museum in the grounds of Grove House. The Rotunda was officially opened by Sir Albert Richardson in 1962, and included a spiral staircase from the recently demolished St James's Theatre.

Her second major book, *The Vivien Greene Dolls' House Collection*, was published by Cassell in 1995.

Three years later, when Vivien was 93 and her eyesight was deteriorating, she decided to auction her collection, and it was sold by Bonham's in two lots in December 1998 and May 1999. Most of the dolls' houses finished up in private hands, but some are still in the public domain.

One is the rather splendid Whiteway, currently on display at Saltram, a Georgian manor owned by the Parker family for nearly 250 years before being acquired by the National Trust in 1959.

The provenance of the dolls' house is something of a mystery. It has been traditionally associated with the real Whiteway at nearby Chudleigh, which became another seat of the Parker family in 1770, but it is not clear where this idea came from. A former curator at Saltram, Patrick Dawes, suggested to Vivien that it had been made for Emily Katherine Parker, daughter of Edmund, 2nd Earl of Morley and his wife (and cousin) Harriet Parker, who inherited Whiteway after her parents' death, but no evidence has been found to support this.

Physically, the dolls' house bears little resemblance to its red-brick namesake, and is much more like Saltram. Although made in 1850, it is Georgian in appearance: a plainer version of Saltram, with three storeys, symmetrically placed rectangular windows, simple balustrade and unadorned central pediment.

Inside, though, the house is largely Victorian. In a letter to Vivien, Dawes tells her that 'the dolls' house was considered an item of outstanding merit by all the members of the staff at Saltram' (*The Vivien Green Dolls' House Collection*, Cassell, 1995). It's easy to see why. The six main rooms are filled with luxurious furnishings, marble-effect fireplaces, ornate mirrors and picture frames, patterned carpets and objets d'art. It has a general air of comfortable, gracious living.

One of the highlights is the library, which has fitted wooden bookshelves – a rarity in Victorian houses – and the tiny books are all made of wood. The drawing room, with its light blue silk wallpaper, edged with gilt metal, comfortable seating and Evans and Cartwright pedestal table, has an overall effect of light and space. In contrast, the dining room is decorated in red, from the red quilted silk lining the walls to the plush red carpet and red-patterned curtains. On the table is a set of imitation Meissen china.

The nursery is typically Victorian with its array of fun and educational toys, many of them added by Vivien. These include a toy theatre, a castle, model houses and a wooden horse, and there is a globe on one of the side tables.

According to Vivien, Montagu Brownlow Parker, the 5th Earl of Morley, gave the dolls' house to his footman's daughter after assuming ownership of Saltram in 1951. It later finished up on the antiques market, and Vivien was able to add it to her collection. It was donated to the National Trust in 1998.

Another house formerly owned by Vivien Greene is The Original Swan, now on display at Ilkely Toy Museum in Yorkshire. The house dates from around 1865–70 and at one time belonged to a lady in Abingdon, Oxfordshire. It was later converted into a 'family and commercial hotel', its name based on a public house in Cowley, Oxford, close to Vivien's home at Iffley. Some of the furnishings shown in *The Vivien Greene Dolls' House Collection* seem to have been lost, but the bar still has its specially made mahogany serving bar, glass bottles and wooden barrel, and there are still curtains and various bits of other furniture in the other rooms.

An obvious addition from Vivien is the sign over the front door reading: 'H.G. Greene is licensed to sell beer, wines and spirits, and tobacco to be consumed on the premises'.

You can almost imagine her chuckling as she assigns this new employment to her errant husband.

Vivien died in 2003 and her beloved Oxford home was sold. Even now, though, its distinctive round tower catches the eye as you drive down the Iffley Road towards Oxford city centre, a reminder that this was once a haven for a cornucopia of miniature delights.

Mary Greg

Mary Greg is one of the unsung heroes of the dolls' house world. Her name is little known, yet she was one of the early benefactors of the V&A Museum of Childhood at Bethnal Green, home to the UK's premier dolls' house collection. Flora Gill Jacobs credits Mary with being 'one of the first collectors to perceive the importance of dolls' houses and their furnishings' (*A History of Dolls' Houses*, Bell & Hyman, 1965), while Margaret Towner hailed her as 'the most discriminating collector before the Second World War' (*The Vivien Greene Dolls' House Collection*, Cassell, 1995).

She was born Mary Hope on 1 March 1850 to Thomas Arthur Hope (1817–1897) and Emily Hird Jones (1818–1887), and was one of twelve children. Recognising that many traditional crafts were dying out as industrialisation increased its grip, she developed a passion for traditional, handcrafted items and over many years she collected a wide range of domestic bygones, from clothes, shoes and other textiles to toys and sewing equipment.

In 1895, aged 45, she married Thomas Tylston Greg (1858–1920), whose family founded the pioneering cotton mill at Quarry Bank near Wilmslow, Cheshire, in 1784. Thomas had eschewed the family business to become a solicitor in Kensington, and in his leisure time he was an art lover, a collector of porcelain and a connoisseur of fine wine. He also clearly possessed a sense of humour, because during the 1890s he wrote several witty, light-hearted essays on drink for the *Pall Mall Gazette* and the *National Observer,* later collected and published under the title *Through a Glass Lightly: Confession of a Reluctant Water Drinker* (Pushkin Press, 1897).

The marriage was a meeting of minds; Mary and Thomas shared a passion for collecting beautiful, interesting and valuable objects, and both had the same philanthropic attitude. When Thomas inherited his uncle's estate in Hertfordshire in 1906, he donated his porcelain collection to the City of Manchester Art Gallery. On 23 February the same year, he gave a lecture at the gallery entitled *A Contribution to the History of English Pottery With Special Reference to the Greg Collection*, and this was published by the gallery in 1908, the original copies being priced at tuppence.

Tragically, Thomas died in 1920, aged just 62, having never recovered from the loss of one of his nephews during the First World War.

The newly widowed Mary coped with her grief by involving herself more closely with her collections and developing connections with various museums. Around this time, the V&A Museum at Bethnal Green, which had been established in 1872, was trying to relaunch itself as a children's museum under the direction of new curator Arthur Sabin. Inspired by the success of a temporary exhibition for children during 1915–16, Sabin's vision was to create permanent displays and activities that would be of interest to children.

When Mary heard about Sabin's project she donated some of her toy collection, and continued to do so over many years. One of the most historically important donations was the Nuremberg Kitchen (see page 49), which dates from the early nineteenth century. Other contributions included Caroline Cottage, made in 1831 by an estate carpenter for 6-year-old Caroline Gordon of Abergeldie Castle in Aberdeenshire, and Spooner Cottage, a model of a country cottage and garden that Mary commissioned for the museum in 1924 from architect Charles Spooner.

Mary also donated a large number of dolls' houses, miniature shops and another Nuremberg Kitchen to the Manchester Art Gallery. Most of the houses date from the nineteenth century, with one dating from the late eighteenth century. An unusual item in the collection is the Frog House, a two-storey, glass-fronted house dating from around 1840, which is populated by stuffed frogs! Sadly, Mary's collection is currently in storage in the Manchester Art Gallery's conservation studios at Harpurhey, with no immediate plans to put any of the models back on display. This seems to have been the fate of this collection for some years – as far back as 1965, Flora Gill Jacobs recorded in *A History of Dolls' Houses* that Mary's dolls' houses at Manchester were in storage.

Several other museums benefited from Mary's generosity, including the Geffrye Museum in London and the British Museum.

Mary died at Sedgley on 15 September 1949, just six months short of her 100th birthday, and she was cremated at Perry Bar Crematorium, Birmingham, on 20 September. Her ashes were buried at Westmill Church, Buntingford, Hertfordshire, with her husband, and there is a memorial tablet to Mary and Thomas in the church.

Patrick Murray

Patrick Murray reputedly disliked children – and yet he was responsible for opening the first museum in the world to shine a spotlight on the social history of childhood. Incongruous maybe, but as Murray explained, this was 'not a children's museum; it is a museum about them'.

Today, the Museum of Childhood in Edinburgh is both a shrine to childhood and a tribute to Patrick Murray's energy, vision and determination.

Born in 1908, Murray was an optician by trade and also a local councillor who served on the Libraries and Museums Committee. After discovering that two dolls once belonging to Queen Victoria were being sent to London because there was nowhere to display them in Scotland, he resolved to start a museum in the heart of Scotland's historic capital city. He persuaded his fellow committee members to allow him some display space at Lady Stair's Museum, just off Edinburgh's famous Royal Mile, in the building now occupied by The Writers Museum.

The museum opened in 1955 with a collection of Murray's own childhood toys, which he disparagingly described as 'a pitiful handful of soldiers, building blocks and railway stuff'. The collection may have been sparse, but it captured people's interest. Before long, Murray was inundated as people generously donated their own childhood treasures, and within a couple of years the collection had outgrown its first modest home.

On 16 August 1957, the museum officially reopened in a converted eighteenth-century tenement building on the Royal Mile, and five years later Murray resigned from the local council to become the museum's first full-time curator.

He soon proved himself to be a man of many talents with a shrewd business sense, clever marketing skills and a flair for effective and imaginative layout of the museum. He also had a mischievous sense of humour, penning quirky captions for the exhibits. The caption for a mid-nineteenth century mechanical bear, for instance, read:

> What with the passage of the years, to say nothing of the hazards of nursery life, it is now impossible to obtain a clear idea of what the toy did in its prime. At present (1961) its outlook is obstinate.

Murray also liked to play on his reputation for disliking children. Asked by a radio interviewer whether he liked children, he replied, 'Not between meals', and once declared that, 'children are only tolerable after their baths and on their way to bed'. More controversially, he once displayed a design in the museum's entrance hall for a proposed memorial window to 'good' King Herod, which was captioned:

> Modern research suggests that the exact number of 'Innocents' massacred could not have been more than twelve or fifteen. To a Museum Curator, when distracted by noisy or aggravating children, this seems a very disappointing total, and one well within his capacities to improve.

It is not difficult to imagine the howls of outrage that would greet such a caption today.

Murray was awarded an MBE for services to museums in 1972, and retired two years later, aged 74. He died in 1981, but his collection continued to grow, eventually expanding into an adjacent building that had once been a Georgian theatre (the ceiling of which can still be seen on the first floor) and later an ironmonger's.

The collection now occupies five floors, and is a treasure chest of childhood memories. The museum's evocative displays of toys and artefacts reflect all aspects of childhood, from infancy, schooldays, children at work and children's clothes to a vast assortment of toys: push-along toys, trains, model vehicles, toy soldiers, farms and zoos, mechanical toys, optical toys, puppets, toy theatres, teddy bears, dolls, board games and outdoor toys.

Included in the collection, of course, is a large number of dolls' houses, including Stanbrig Eorls (see Chapter 4) and the 1930s Triang house Y Bwythn Bach (see Chapter 5).

Other dolls' houses in the collection include a Tudor-style Triang house from the 1930s, an 1870s Stockbridge house from West End, Edinburgh, and an early twentieth-century plywood house. There are also model shops and room settings, including a Nuremberg kitchen from 1900 and a late nineteenth century butcher's shop, as well as miniature dolls, tea sets and furniture. Of particular note is a set of finely crafted ivory furniture from the nineteenth century, as well as some wooden furniture from the 1930s made by South Lanarkshire craftsman James Fleming.

Another highlight is a pair of rooms filled with items that were originally created for a Miniaturists' Competition and displayed at a Save the Children Fund exhibition in 1982. These include a rocking horse, exquisitely crafted furniture and assorted smaller items. The lower room features a Queen Anne walnut desk, made to commemorate the wedding of Prince Charles and Lady Diana Spencer in 1981 by Bridlington craftsman John J. Hodgson, best known for his model houses at Hever Castle (see Chapter 6).

If Patrick Murray could see the museum today, and see how much his collection has grown from that 'pitiful handful' of toys, he would no doubt be proud.

Charles Paget Wade

Architect, artist, craftsman and inveterate hoarder Charles Paget Wade began the collecting habit early. Snowshill Manor in Gloucestershire, his former home, became a collector's paradise and now, under the ownership of the National Trust, it is a shrine to his insatiable appetite for the artistic and the curious. Among this stash of artistically arranged treasures can be found three dolls' houses and buildings from a model village.

Born in Yoxford, Suffolk, in 1883, Wade was sent to live with his grandmother, Katherine Spencer, at the age of 7 so that he could attend the local preparatory school as a day pupil. There, as he recalled in his memoirs *Days Far Away*, he became fascinated with 'an exceptionally lovely Chinese cabinet of black and gold lacquer'. This cabinet 'was my greatest joy and its fascination never failed'.

The cabinet was only opened on Sundays, and the young Charles used to relish those magical moments when his grandmother revealed the 'interesting old family treasures' behind the lavishly decorated doors.

Wade was inspired to buy small treasures of his own with his pocket money, and over the next couple of decades he gradually amassed a miscellany of objects, large and small, from all over the world. A champion of the Arts and Crafts movement, he made a point of collecting traditional, hand-crafted items, writing in 1945: 'What joy these old things are to live with, each piece made by the hand of craftsmen, each has a feeling and individuality that no machine could ever attain.'

In 1919 Wade found a place for his collection: a derelict, ninth-century manor tucked away in the heart of the Cotswolds. Wade restored the house and grounds with the help of fellow architect M.H. Baillie Scott and a team of twenty-eight workmen, and Snowshill Manor became his own 'cabinet of curiosities', every piece carefully and sympathetically placed. As the collection grew, Wade moved into an old priest's cottage in the grounds and allowed his treasures to take over the main house.

By the time Wade presented the manor and its contents to the National Trust in 1951, his collection had spread into nineteen rooms, each of which was given a whimsical name according to its contents and position in the house.

In 'Seventh Heaven', among Wade's childhood toys, is the oldest and smallest dolls' house in the collection: a Georgian townhouse that once belonged to Wade's mother, Amy Blanche Spencer (born 1858). Standing just 48cm (1ft 7in) high and less than a foot wide, this simple wooden box is divided into two rooms, one up and one down, each featuring a central fireplace, some plain wooden furniture and white wallpaper decorated with green leaves and daisies.

The red-brick exterior bears a fire mark for Sun, one of the insurance companies set up in the aftermath of the Great Fire of London. The fire mark or 'plate', which identified insured buildings to the fire brigades, became redundant after ten insurance companies amalgamated in 1833 to form the London Fire Engine Establishment (LFEE).

In *Days Far Away*, Wade fondly describes his mother's dolls' house:

How inviting it looked, the front so trim, so prim. How neat the red brick walls ... The white barred sash windows of real glass so evenly spaced. The wide friendly door of emerald green with a brass lion knocker, white painted architrave and circular fanlight above. On the doorstep, red pots with gay flowers, a foot scraper on the side.

In 'Mermaid' are two dolls' houses. One, a 5ft-high house dating from 1800, appears to have been assembled by the amalgamation of three separate display cases. The single top storey contains a motley collection of wooden, wax and ceramic dolls of various sizes, with tiny figures, animals and toys at their feet. The lower storey is divided equally into two, one of which is occupied by another curious assemblage of dolls, soft toys, tiny lead soldiers and two wooden marionettes in Eastern dress.

The other section contains a favourite relic from Wade's childhood: a grocer's shop with an assortment of tiny jars, tins and boxes, as well as some wooden drawers that the young Charles used to fill with 'real tea, rice, coffee, cloves, lentils, sugar and spice'. The proprietor is 'Robert, a remarkable man, most efficient, for he had no assistant save a quite mythical errand boy'. Robert's main customers were from 'my sister's two dolls' houses'.

The most splendid of the dolls' house collection is a three-storey model made by Wade around 1907 for Elizabeth Murray (known as Betty), the 4-year-old daughter of author Kate Murray. Wade was later to illustrate one of Kate Murray's books, *The Spirit of the House* (Hodder & Stoughton, 1915) with colour drawings and a fold-out plan of the house, and the two families frequently socialised at Snowshill and at the Murray home.

The dolls' house was inhabited by the imaginary Lord Mex and his family. A fairly simple design, it has a plain red roof with a chimney at either end, fronted by a pediment with ox-eye window. The furniture is all nineteenth century, and was probably collected by Wade over a number of years. The house illustrates the typical Victorian divide between the family and their servants, with the lavish, over-cluttered rooms above stairs contrasting with the austerity of those below. A highlight is the ornament-filled display case, made from wood and covered with varnished black and gold paper featuring lions' faces, cherub pillars and geometric patterns. Nearby are matching chairs, coffee table and dressing table. This contrasts with the plain wooden furniture in the ground floor rooms.

Wade's other miniature triumph was his model village, Wolf's Cove, believed to be the first of its kind in Britain. It predates its more famous cousin, Bekonscot, by around twenty years, having started in 1908 at Hampstead, his former home, as a Gauge 1 garden railway and a few rural buildings for the amusement of Betty Murray. Originally called Fladbury, the village came to Snowshill with Wade in 1919 and gradually expanded around a purpose-built pond in the garden, becoming more like a Cornish fishing village than a rural railway and earning its change of name to Wolf's Cove.

In its heyday, the detailed craftsmanship and realism of Wolf's Cove attracted a great deal of interest. John Betjeman – one of Wade's many celebrity guests at Snowshill – was so impressed by Wolf's Cove that in 1932 he wrote a detailed description for *Architectural Review*, only revealing at the end of the article that he had been writing about a 1/2 scale model.

The original Wolf's Cove buildings are now displayed indoors to prevent deterioration, but in 2010 the National Trust began recreating the village based on photographs and documents from the archives. This is now on display during the summer.

In 1946, Wade married Mary Graham, the daughter of a Leicestershire vicar. When the couple moved to St Kitts in 1951, Wade handed Snowshill over to the National Trust. He died in July 1956, aged 73, and was buried at Snowshill Church alongside his mother and sisters.

Appendix 1

Places to Visit

Below is a comprehensive (but not exhaustive) list of museums, historic homes and other places in the UK and overseas featuring collections of dolls' houses and miniatures, plus a selection of model villages. All details are correct at the time of writing, but displays do change so it is always advisable to check before you visit. At the end are details of dolls' house shops and dolls' house fairs and festivals.

England

Berkshire
Legoland Windsor
Winkfield Road, Windsor SL4 4AY
Tel: 08714 232280
www.legoland.co.uk
Includes the miniature park Miniland.

Windsor Castle
Windsor, Berkshire SL4 1NJ
www.rct.uk/visit/windsorcastle
Queen Mary's dolls' house – the world's largest dolls' house.

Buckinghamshire
Amersham Museum
49 High Street, Amersham, Bucks HP7 0DP
Tel: 01494 723700

Email: info@amershammuseum.org
www.amershammuseum.org
Dolls' house and other wooden toys by Amersham Toys, plus
two Triang houses and a Georgian-style house.

Bekonscot Model Village
Warwick Road, Beaconsfield, Buckinghamshire HP9 2PL
Tel: 01494 672919
Email: info@bekonscot.co.uk
www.bekonscot.co.uk
The oldest and most famous model village in continuous existence.

Bucks County Museum
Church Street, Aylesbury HP20 2QP
Tel: 01296 331441
Email: museum@buckscountymuseum.org
www.buckscountymuseum.org
Locally made dolls' house from 1845 and a dolls' house made as
a money box in 1927.

Cambridgeshire
The Museum of Cambridge
2-3 Castle Street, Cambridge CB3 0AQ
Tel: 01223 355159
www.folkmuseum.org.uk
Several dolls' houses in the collection; not all on display.

Wimpole Hall (National Trust)
Wimpole Estate, Arrington, Royston, Cambs SG8 0BW
Tel: 01223 206000
Email: wimpolehall@nationaltrust.org.uk
www.nationaltrust.org.uk/wimpole-estate
Dolls' house dating from 1930s; donated to the National Trust
in 1996.

Cheshire
Dunham Massey (National Trust)
Altrincham, Cheshire WA14 4SJ

Tel: 01619 411025
Email: dunhammassey@nationaltrust.org.uk
www.nationaltrust.org.uk/dunham-massey
Small dolls' house with two rooms and thatched roof, date unknown.

Manchester Art Gallery
Mosley Street, Manchester M2 3JL
Tel: 0161 235 8888
Email: online form
www.manchesterartgallery.org
Collection of dolls' houses and shops given to the museum by
Mary Greg in 1934; currently in storage.

Cornwall
Lanhydrock
Bodmin, Cornwall PL30 5AD
Tel: 01208 265950
Email: lanhydrock@nationaltrust.org.uk
www.nationaltrust.org.uk/lanhydrock
Three-storey dolls' house by Lines Brothers, transferred from
Berrington Hall in 1994.

Polperro Model Village & Land of Legend
Mill Hill, Polperro, Cornwall PL13 2RP
Tel: 01503 272378
Email: online form
www.polperromodelvillage.co.uk
Recreation of Polperro, established in the late 1940s.

County Durham
Bowes Museum
Barnard Castle, Co. Durham DL12 8NP
Tel: 01833 690606
Email: info@thebowesmuseum.org.uk
www.thebowesmuseum.org.uk
Small dolls' house made by William Dobson, a colliery labourer
from Barnard Castle, dating from c.1840.

<u>Cumbria</u>
Hill Top
Near Sawrey, Hawkshead, Ambleside, Cumbria LA22 0LF
Tel: 01539 436269
Email: hilltop@nationaltrust.org.uk
www.nationaltrust.org.uk/hill-top
Dolls' house containing the food and other items stolen by Hunca
Munca and Tom Thumb in *The Tale of the Two Bad Mice*.

A World in Miniature Museum
Houghton Hall Garden Centre, Houghton, Carlisle, Cumbria
CA6 4JB
Tel: 01228 400610
Email: houghtonhall@klondyke.co.uk
www.klondyke.co.uk/houghton-hall-garden-centre-carlisle
Large collection of room settings containing 1/12 scale copies of
antique furniture, paintings, ornaments and everyday domestic items.

<u>Derbyshire</u>
Calke Abbey
Ticknall, Derby DE73 1LE
Tel: 01332 853822
Email: calkeabbey@nationaltrust.org.uk
www.nationaltrust.org.uk
Three Victorian dolls' houses, one converted to a weather house.

Old House Museum Bakewell
Cunningham Place, North Church Street, Bakewell, Derbyshire
DE45 1DD
Tel: 01629 813642
Email: bakewellmuseum@gmail.com
www.oldhousemuseum.org.uk
Several dolls' houses from different eras, plus a butcher's shop.

National Trust Museum of Childhood
Sudbury Hall and the National Trust Museum of Childhood
Main Road, Sudbury, Ashbourne, Derbyshire DE6 5HT

Tel: 01283 585337
Email: sudburyhall@nationaltrust.org.uk
www.nationaltrust.org.uk/sudbury-hall-and-the-national-trust-museum-of-childhood
Major collection of dolls' houses and other miniatures, not all on permanent display. Includes items from the Betty Cadbury collection.

Devon
All Hallows Museum of Lace and Local Antiquities
High Street, Honiton, Devon EX14 1PG
Tel: 01404 44966
Email: info@honitonmuseum.co.uk
www.honitonmuseum.co.uk
Mid-Victorian furnished dolls' house.

Babbacombe Model Village
Hampton Avenue, Babbacombe, Torquay, Devon TQ1 3LA
Tel: 01803 315315
Email: mail@model-village.co.uk
www.model-village.co.uk
Established in 1963, now one of the largest of its kind.

Bickleigh Castle Museum
Tiverton, Devon EX16 8RP
Tel: 01884 855363
Email: info@bickleighcastle.com
https://bickleighcastle.com
Two fully furnished dolls' houses, one dating from 1873.

Castle Drogo
Drewsteignton, Exeter, Devon EX6 6PB
Tel: 01647 433306
Email: castledrogo@nationaltrust.org.uk
www.nationaltrust.org.uk/castle-drogo
Large dolls' house from 1820 and a very grand house from 1906 made for 6-year-old Mary Drewe.

Coldharbour Mill
Uffcolme, Cullompton, Devon EX15 3EE
Tel: 01884 840960
Email: info@coldharbourmill.org.uk
www.coldharbourmill.org.uk
Hand-crafted, fully furnished replicas of nineteenth and twentieth-century dolls' houses, each giving a snapshot of family life at a particular moment.

Dawlish Museum
Dawlish Museum Society, The Knowle, Barton Terrace, Dawlish EX7 9QH
Tel: 01626 888557
Email: info@dawlishmuseum.co.uk
www.devonmuseums.net
Restored dolls' house by Mr Gordon McMurtie, plus dolls' house furniture in room settings.

Fairlynch Museum & Arts Centre
27 Fore Street, Budleigh Salterton, Devon EX9 6NP
Tel: 01395 442666
Email: use online form
www.fairlynchmuseum.uk
Home to large collection of dolls, dolls' houses, teddy bears and games from the nineteenth century, but not all on permanent display. Holds annual themed exhibitions.

Overbeck's House (National Trust)
Sharpitor, Salcombe, Devon TQ8 8LW
Tel: 01548 842893
Email: overbecks@nationaltrust.org.uk
www.nationaltrust.org.uk/overbecks
Palladian-style house created in the 1980s by Mabel Hill.

Saltram (National Trust)
Plympton, Plymouth, Devon PL7 1UH
Tel: 01752 333500
Email: saltram@nationaltrust.org.uk

www.nationaltrust.org.uk/saltram
Whiteways dolls' house, dating from c1850 and originally part of the Vivien Greene collection.

Topsham Museum
25 Strand, Topsham, Exeter EX3 0AX
Tel: 01392 873244
Email: info@topshammuseum.org.uk
www.topshammuseum.org.net
Georgian-style dolls' house modelled on Wear House (now Exeter Golf & Country Club).

Totnes Elizabethan House Museum
70 Fore Street, Totnes, Devon TQ9 5RU
Tel: 01803 863821
Email: info@totnesmuseum.org
www.totnesmuseum.org
Victorian nursery with two dolls' houses.

Dorset
Blandford Forum Town Museum
Bere's Yard, Blandford Forum, Dorset DT11 7HQ
Tel: 01258 450388
Email: blandfordtownmuseum@uwclub.net
http://blandfordtownmuseum.org.uk
Georgian-style dolls' house made by Charles de Lacy in the nineteenth century, with handmade furniture and other items reflecting his own home, family and domestic staff. Added to by subsequent generations.

Corfe Castle Model Village
The Square, Corfe Castle, Dorset BH20 5EZ
Tel: 01929 481234
Email: info@corfecastlemodelvillage.co.uk
www.corfecastlemodelvillage.co.uk
A miniature recreation of Corfe Castle village as it looked in the mid-seventeenth century.

Sherborne Museum
Church Lane, Sherborne, Dorset DT9 3BP
Tel: 01935 812252
Email; info@sherbornemuseum.co.uk
www.sherbornemuseum.co.uk
Dolls' house from nineteenth century.

Wimborne Model Town
King Street, Wimborne Minster, Dorset BH21 1DY
Tel: 01202 881924
Email: info@wimborne-modeltown.com
www.wimborne-modeltown.com
Recreation of Wimborne in the 1950s. Includes the Beryl Dade
Dolls' House Collection.

Essex
Audley End House and Gardens (English Heritage)
Off London Road, Saffron Walden, Essex CB11 4JF
Tel: 01799 522842
www.english-heritage.org.uk/visit/places/audley-end-house-
and-gardens
Dolls' house reflecting domestic life at Audley End in the early
nineteenth century.

Hollytrees Museum
Castle Park, Colchester, Essex CO1 1UG
Tel: 01206 282940
Email: museums@colchester.gov
https://Colchester.cimuseums.org.uk/visit/hollytrees-museum
Four-storey Georgian dolls' house

House on the Hill Toy Museum
Stansted Mountfitchet, Essex CM24 8SP
Tel: 01279 813237
Email: info@stanstedtoymuseum.com
www.stanstedtoymuseum.com
Several dolls' houses on display.

Gloucestershire
The Model Village
The Old New Inn, Bourton-on-the-Water, Gloucestershire
GL54 2AF
Tel: 01451 820467
Email: bourtonmodelvillage@theoldnewinn.co.uk
www.themodelvillage.com
Model village, Miniature Landscape Exhibition and Exhibition
of Miniatures.

Snowshill Manor and Garden (National Trust)
Snowshill, Nr Broadway, Gloucestershire WR12 7JU
Tel: 01386 852410
Email: snowshillmanor@nationaltrust.org.uk
www.nationaltrust.org.uk/snowshill-manor-and-garden
Three dolls' houses, from the eighteenth, nineteenth and early
twentieth centuries, plus the model village Wolf's Cove.

Hampshire
Fordingbridge Museum
King's Yard, Salisbury Street, Fordingbridge, Hants SP6 1AB
Tel: 01425 655222
Email: info@fordingbridgemuseum.co.uk
www.fordingbridgemuseum.co.uk
Large Victorian furnished dolls house.

Southsea Model Village
Lumps Fort, Eastney Esplanade, Southsea, Hampshire PO4
9RU
Tel: 02392 751443
Email: southseamodelvillage@hotmail.com
www.southseamodelvillage.biz
1/12 scale model village dating from 1956.

Herefordshire
The Time Machine Museum of Science Fiction
12 The Square, Bromyard, Herefordshire HR7 4BP

Tel: 01885 488329
Email: info@timemachineuk.com
www.timemachine.com
Two fully furnished Victorian dolls' houses.

Hertfordshire
Dolls House Exhibition
Maple Street Dolls Houses and Miniatures
Maple Street, Wendy, Royston, Herts SG8 0AB
Tel: 01223 207025
Email: info@maplestreet.co.uk
www.maplestreet.co.uk/pages/exhibition.htm
Exhibition of dolls' houses, period room boxes, the Dawn
Lockyer collection and Patricia Labistour's Music in Miniature
exhibition.

North Herts Museum
Brand Street, Hitchin, Herts SG5 1JE
Tel: 01462 474554
Email: northhertsmuseum@north-herts.gov.uk
www.north-herts.gov.uk/museum
Victorian dolls' house.

Isle of Wight
The Model Village
High Street, Godshill, Isle of Wight PO38 3HH
Tel: 01983 840270
Email: hello@modelvillagegodshill.co.uk
www.modelvillagegodshill.co.uk
Recreation of Godshill and the nearby town of Shanklin as they
appeared in the 1930s.

Osborne House (English Heritage)
York Avenue, East Cowes, Isle of Wight PO32 6JX
Tel: 01983 200022
www.english-heritage.org.uk/visit/places/osborne
Dolls' house in nursery played with by Queen Victoria's children.

Kent
Beaney House of Art and Knowledge
18 High Street, Canterbury, Kent CT1 2RA
Tel: 01227 862162
Email: beaney@canterbury.gov.uk
www.canterburymuseums.co.uk/beaney/materials-and-masters/dolls-house
Dolls and dolls' house furniture from early twentieth century, collected by Miss G.H. Veraguth (1880–1974), selected and arranged by artist and puppeteer Estelle Rosenfeld.

Hever Castle and Gardens
Hever, Edenbridge, Kent TN8 7NG
Tel: 01732 865224
Email: info@hevercastle.co.uk
www.hevercastle.co.uk
Miniature Model Houses exhibition, reflecting different eras of domestic life from medieval to Victorian.

Maidstone Museum & Art Gallery
St Faith's Street, Maidstone, Kent ME14 1LH
Tel: 01622 602838
Email: museuminfo@maidstone.gov.uk
https://museum.maidstone.gov.uk
Collection of dolls' houses dating from the early nineteenth to the late twentieth centuries.

Penshurst Place Toy Museum
Penshurst, Tonbridge, Kent TN11 8DG
Tel: 01892 870307
Email: enquiries@penshurstplace.com
www.penshurstplace.com
Toy museum includes several dolls' houses from the nineteenth and twentieth centuries.

Tunbridge Wells Museum & Art Gallery
Civic Centre, Mount Pleasant, Royal Tunbridge Wells, Kent TN1 1JN

Tel: 01892 554171
Email: museum@tunbridgewells.gov.uk
www.tunbridgewellsmuseum.org
Collections include the Rigg dolls' house from c.1840. Not currently on display due to refurbishment; reopening 2021.

Lancashire
Hoghton Tower
Hoghton, Nr Preston, Lancs PR5 0SH
Tel: 01254 852986
Email: mail@hoghtontower.co.uk
www.hoghtontower.co.uk
Collection of dolls' houses from the nineteenth and twentieth centuries.

Rufford Old Hall (National Trust)
200 Liverpool Road, Rufford, Nr Ormskirk, Lancs L40 1SG
Tel: 01704 821254
Email: ruffordoldhall@nationaltrust.org.uk
www.nationaltrust.org.uk/rufford-old-hall
Dolls' house from c1890.

Lincolnshire
Belton House (National Trust)
Grantham, Lincs NG32 2LS
Tel: 01476 566116
Email: belton@nationaltrust.org.uk
www.nationaltrust.org.uk/belton-house
Wooden dolls' house, date unknown.

London
2 Willow Road (National Trust)
Hampstead, London NW3 1TH
Nearest underground station: Hampstead (Northern Line)
Tel: 020 7435 6166
Email: 2willowroad@nationaltrust.org.uk

www.nationalstrust.org.uk/2-willow-road
Former home of designer Erno Goldfinger includes the dolls'
house he made for his daughter in the 1940s.

Charles Dickens Museum
48-49 Doughty Street, London WC1N 2LX
Nearest underground station: Russell Square
Tel: 020 7405 2127
Email: info@dickensmuseum.com
https://dickensmuseum.com
Dolls' house modelled on the museum building, built by Christopher
Cole for his 1976 book *Make Your Own Dolls' House.*

Gunnersbury Park Museum
Gunnersbury, Popes Lane, London W5 4NH
Nearest underground station: Acton Town (Piccadilly & District
lines)
Tel: 020 3961 0280
Email: info@visitgunnersbury.org
www.visitgunnersbury.org
Two fully furnished Victorian dolls' houses.

Horniman Museum
100 London Road, Forest Hill, London SE23 3PQ
London Overground station: Forest Hill
Tel: 020 8699 1872
Email: enquiry@horniman.ac.uk
www.horniman.ac.uk
English nineteenth-century dolls' house and Japanese twentieth-
century dolls' house on display on the 'Sentiments Wall' in the
World Gallery, both fully furnished and decorated.

Jewish Museum London
Raymond Burton House, 129-131 Albert Street, London NW1 7NB
Nearest underground station: Camden Town (Northern line)
Tel: 020 7284 7384

Email: admin@jewishmuseum.org.uk
https://jewishmuseum.org.uk
Thelma's dolls' house.

Kew Palace
Royal Botanic Gardens Kew, Richmond TW9 3AE
Nearest underground station: Kew Gardens (District Line)
Tel: 020 8332 5655
Email: info@kew.org
www.kew.org
Dolls' house made for the daughters of King George III.

Museum of London
150 London Wall, London EC2Y 5HN
Nearest underground station: Barbican (Metropolitan or Circle
Line) or St Paul's (Central Line)
Tel: 020 7001 9844
Email: online form
www.museumoflondon.org.uk
Blackett baby house on display in Expanding City Gallery.

Pollock's Toy Museum
1 Scala Street, London W1T 2HL (entrance is at 41, Whitfield
Street)
Nearest underground station: Goodge Street (Northern Line)
Tel: 020 7636 3452
Email: pollockstoymuseum@gmail.com
www.pollockstoys.com
Numerous dolls' houses, mainly from the nineteenth and
twentieth centuries, plus model shops, room settings and toy
theatres.

V&A Museum of Childhood
Cambridge Heath Road, Bethnal Green, London E2 9PA
Nearest underground station: Bethnal Green (Central Line)
Tel: 020 8983 5200
Email: moc@vam.ac.uk

www.vam.ac.uk/moc
Largest collection of dolls' houses in the UK, spanning more than 300 years.

Merseyside
Southport Model Railway Village
Lower Promenade, Kings Gardens, Southport, Merseyside PR8 1QX
Tel: 01704 538001
Email: spmodrailvillage@aol.com
www.southportmodelrailwayvillage.co.uk
Model village and railway reflecting architecture of Merseyside and South West Lancashire.

Norfolk
Bishop Bonner's Cottage Museum
St Withburga Lane, Dereham NR19 1ED
www.derehamhistory.com/museum.html
Includes the Alan Cambridge Hobbies collection.

Gressenhall Farm & Workhouse Museum of Norfolk Life
Gressenhall, Dereham, Norfolk NR20 4DR
Tel: 01362 860563
Email: gressenhall.museum@norfolk.gov.uk
www.museums.norfolk.gov.uk/gressenhall-farm-and-workhouse
Wooden architectural model of Melton Constable Hall, Norfolk, dating from the seventeenth century; the oldest surviving model of its kind in Britain.

Museum of Norwich at the Bridewell
Bridewell Abbey, Norwich NR2 1AQ
Tel: 01603 629127
Email: museums@norfolk.gov.uk
www.museums.norfolk.gov.uk/museum-of-norwich
Spitfire Cottage made by sisters Philippa Miller and Pamela Baker during the Second World War.

Norfolk Museums Service
Tel: 01603 493625
Email: museums@norfolk.gov.uk
www.museums.norfolk.gov.uk
Baby house from c.1740, a replica of 27 King Street, King's
Lynn. Not currently on display.

Wroxham Miniature Worlds
Station Business Park, Horning Road West, Hoveton, Norfolk
NR12 8QJ
Tel: 01603 781728
Email: info@wroxhamminiatureworlds.co.uk
www.wroxhamminiatureworlds.co.uk
Attractions include Dolls World, a collection of dolls' houses and
other exhibits by local artist Sue Wylie, donated by her family
after her death from cancer in 2014.

Northumberland
Cragside (National Trust)
Rothbury, Morpeth, Northumberland NE65 7PX
Tel: 01669620333
Email: cragside@nationaltrust.org.uk
www.nationaltrust.org.uk/cragside
Dolls' house with roof and blue door, date unknown. Not
currently on display.

Wallington
Cambo, near Morpeth, Northumberland NE61 4AR
Tel: 01670 773600
Email: wallington@nationaltrust.org.uk
www.nationaltrust.org.uk/wallington
Collection of eighteen dolls' houses, the oldest of which dates
back to 1835. Includes the Hammond House.

Nottinghamshire
Museum of Nottingham Life at Brewhouse Yard
Castle Boulevard, Nottingham NG7 1FB

Tel: 01158 761400
Email: online form
www.nottinghamcastle.org.uk/
Dolls' house donated to the museum in 2003. Museum currently
closed for redevelopment.

Oxfordshire
Banbury Museum
Spiceball Park Road, Banbury, Oxon OX16 2PQ
Tel: 01295 753752
Email: enquiries@banburymuseum.org
www.banburymuseum.org
Late nineteenth-century wooden dolls' house, fully furnished,
with three dolls made by Simon and Halbig in Germany c.1900–
30. Displays include other toys and dolls from the eighteenth to
the twentieth centuries.

Fairytale Farm
Southcombe, Chipping Norton, Oxon OX7 5QH
Tel: 01608 238014
Email: info@fairytalefarm.co.uk
Website: www.fairytalefarm.co.uk
Tiny model village with resident mice!

Grey's Court
Rotherfield Greys, Henley-on-Thames, Oxon RG9 4PG
Tel: 01491 628529
Email: greyscourt@nationaltrust.org.uk
www.nationaltrust.org.uk/greys-court
The Havercroft Mackenzie dolls' house, created in the 1970s by
Patricia Mackenzie to represent the 1860s.

Oxfordshire Museum
Fletcher's House, Park Street, Woodstock, Oxon OX20 1SN
Tel: 01993 814106
Email: oxonmuseum@oxfordshire.gov.uk
www.oxfordshire.gov.uk/museums

Three-storey, white painted wooden dolls' house from c1860. Originally belonged to a family in Headington, Oxford, and was later displayed at Cogges Manor Farm near Witney. Other toys from the Victorian era also on display, including a Noah's Ark.

Pendon Museum
Long Wittenham, Abingdon, Oxon OX14 4QD
Tel: 01865 407365 (for opening times), 01865 408143 (office)
Email: info@pendonmuseum.com
https://pendonmuseum.com
Model railways and miniature landscapes representing the 1930s.

Tolsey Museum
126 High Street, Burford, Oxon OX18 4QU
Tel: 01993 822178
www.tolseymusemburford.org
Large dolls' house created 1939 by local people to represent the Regency era.

Somerset
Blaise Castle House Museum
Henbury Road, Bristol BS10 7QS
Tel: 0117 903 9818
Email: online form
www.bristolmuseums.org.uk/blaise-castle-house-museum
Several dolls' houses from the nineteenth century; only one is currently on display.

Weston Museum
Burlington Street, Weston-super-Mare BS23 1PR
Tel: 01934 621028
Email: museum@wsm-tc.gov.uk
www.wesetonmuseum.org
Several dolls' houses in Clara's Cottage, reflecting the 1900s.

Tyntesfield (National Trust)
Wraxall, Bristol, North Somerset BS48 1NX
Tel: 01275 461900
Email: tyntesfield@nationaltrust.org.uk
www.nationaltrust.org.uk/tyntesfield
Miniature facsimile copies of *The Times*, as printed for Queen
Mary's dolls' house, plus other miniature items.

Wells and Mendip Museum
8 Cathedral Green, Wells, Somerset BA5 2UE
Tel: 01749 673477
Email: admin@wellsmuseum.org.uk
www.wellsmuseum.org.uk
Baby house in Wells City Gallery.

Staffordshire
The Potteries Museum & Art Gallery
Bethesda Street, Hanley, Stoke-on-Trent ST1 3DW
Tel: 01782 232323
Email: online form
www.stokemuseums.org.uk
Dolls' house completed in 1982 by local craftsman Peter Hall,
based on Barlaston Hall, an eighteenth-century Palladian
country house designed by Sir Robert Taylor.

World of Wedgwood Museum
Wedgwood Drive, Barlaston, Stoke-on-Trent, Staffs ST12 9ER
Tel: 01782 282986
Email: info@worldofwedgewood.com
www.worldofwedgewood.com
Collection includes a miniature tea set made for Queen Mary's dolls'
house in 1924. Queen Mary and King often visited the factory.

Suffolk
Ickworth (National Trust)
The Rotunda, Horringer, Bury St Edmunds, Suffolk IP29 5QE

Tel: 01284 735270
Email: ickworth@nationaltrust.org.uk
www.nationaltrust.org.uk/ickworth
Silber & Fleming-style box back house from 1880 and a fully
furnished dolls' house from 1907.

Surrey
Clandon Park (National Trust)
West Clandon, Guildford, Surrey GU4 7RQ
Tel: 01483 222482
Email: clandonpark@nationaltrust.org.uk
www.nationaltrust.org.uk/clandon-park
Early nineteenth-century dolls' house.

Polesden Lacey (National Trust)
Great Bookham, Nr Dorking, Surrey RH5 6BD
Tel: 01372 452048
Email: polesdenlacey@nationaltrust.org.uk
www.nationaltrust.org.uk/polesden-lacey
One dolls' house, date unknown.

Sussex
Bexhill Museum
Egerton Road, Bexhill-on-Sea, East Sussex TN39 3HL
Tel: 01424 222058
Email: enquiries@bexhillmuseum.co.uk
www.bexhillmuseum.co.uk
Displays include the Izzard Family model railway.

Horsham Museum and Art Gallery
9 Causeway, Horsham, West Sussex RH12 1HE
Tel: 01403 254959
Email: museum@horsham.gov.uk
https://horshammuseum.org
Edwardian dolls' house in the toy gallery.

Hove Museum and Art Gallery
19 New Church Road, Hove BN3 4AB
Tel: 03000 290900
Email: visitor.services@brighton-hove.gov.uk
www.brightonmuseums.org.uk/hove
Several dolls' houses from the nineteenth and twentieth centuries.

Leonardslee Lakes and Gardens
Brighton Road, Lower Beeding, Horsham RH13 6PP
Tel: 01403 220345
Email: info@leonardsleegardens.co.uk
www.leonardsleegardens.co.uk
'Beyond the Dolls' House' exhibition created in 1998 and recently
restored.

Standen House & Garden (National Trust)
West Hoathly Road, East Grinstead, West Sussex RH19 4NE
Tel: 01342 323029
Email: standen@nationaltrust.org.uk
www.nationaltrust.org.uk/standen-house-and-garden
Christian Hacker dolls' house.

Uppark House
South Harting, Petersfield, West Sussex GU31 5QR
Tel: 01730 825415
Email: uppark@nationaltrust.org.uk
www.nationaltrust.org.uk/uppark-house-and-garden
Uppark dolls' house, dating from 1735-40.

Worthing Museum and Art Gallery
Chapel Road, Worthing, West Sussex BN11 1HP
Tel: 01903 239999
Email: museum@worthing.gov.uk
www.worthing.gov.uk
Collections include several dolls' houses and a butcher's shop.

Warwickshire
Charlecote Park (National Trust)
Wellesbourne, Warwick CV35 9ER
Tel: 01789 470277
Email: charlecotepark@nationaltrust.org.uk
www.nationaltrust.org.uk/charlecote-park
Dolls' house made for Emma Fairfax-Lacy in 1950 by Mr Wimbush
of Charlecote; replica of family rectory at Hampton Lacy, built 1712.

West Midlands
Wightwick Manor (National Trust)
Wightwick Bank, Wolverhampton, West Midlands WV6 8EE
(Sat Nav WV6 8BN)
Tel: 01902 761400
Email: wightwickmanor@nationaltrust.org.uk
www.nationaltrust.org.uk/wightwick-manor-and-gardens
Dolls' house and furnishings from 1945, made for Anthea
Mander by her brother, John. Restored 1993.

Wiltshire
The Dolls House Exhibition and Shop
Longleat, Warminster, Wilts BA12 7NW
Tel: 01985 844400
Email: enquiries@longleat.co.uk
www.longleat.co.uk
Two dolls' houses, dating from 1811 and 1870.

Wilton House
Salisbury, Wiltshire SP2 0BJ
Tel: 01722 746700
Email: admin@wiltonhouse.com
www.wiltonhouse.co.uk
Sir Nevile Wilkinson's Pembroke Palace on display in the shop.

Worcestershire
Hanbury Hall (National Trust)
School Road, Hanbury, Droitwich Spa, Worcestershire WR9 7EA

Tel: 01527 821214
Email: hanburyhall@nationaltrust.org.uk
www.nationaltrust.org.uk/hanbury-hall
Dolls' house c.1880 with contents, four drawers in base, painted softwood.

Yorkshire
Bankfield Museum
Akroyd Park, Boothtown Road, Halifax HX3 6HG
Tel: 01422 352334
Email: museums@calderdale.gov.uk
www.museums.calderdale.gov.uk
Dolls' house on display in the Toy Gallery.

Grassington Folk Museum
6 The Square, Grassington, Skipton, North Yorkshire BD23 5AQ
uwmsoc@gmail.com
https://grassingtonfolkmuseum.org.uk
Dolls house with contents from the eighteenth to the twentieth centuries.

Ilkley Toy Museum
Whitton Croft Road, Ilkley, West Yorkshire LS29 9HR
Tel: 01943 603855
Email: ilkleytoymuseum@outlook.com
www.ilkleytoymuseum.co.uk
Large selection of dolls' houses, shops and room settings. Includes The Original Swan from the Vivien Greene collection.

Newby Hall and Gardens
Newby Hall, Ripon, North Yorkshire HG4 5AE (Sat Nav HG4 5AJ)
Tel: 01423 322583
www.newbyhall.com
Includes exhibition of around seventy fully furnished dolls' houses and shops, one of the largest collections in the world.

Nidderdale Museum
11 King Street, Pateley Bridge, Harrogate, North Yorkshire
HG3 5LE
Tel: 01423 711225
Email: info@nidderdalemuseum.com
www.nidderdalemuseum.com
Dolls' house dating from 1891.

Nostell Priory (National Trust)
Doncaster Road, Nostell, Wakefield, Yorkshire WF4 1QE
01924 863892
Email: nostell@nationaltrust.org.uk
www.nationaltrust.org.uk/nostell
Fully furnished dolls' house dating from 1730–40.

Nunnington Hall (National Trust)
Nunnington, Nr York, North Yorkshire YO62 5UY
Tel: 01439 748283
Email: nunningtonhall@nationaltrust.org.uk
www.nationaltrust.org.uk/nunningtonhall
Home to the Carlisle Collection of miniature room settings,
reflecting domestic life over 300 years.

Weston Park Museum
Western Bank, Sheffield S10 2TP
Tel: 0114 278 2600
Email: info@museums-sheffield.org.uk
www.museums-sheffield.org.uk/museums/weston-park/home
Dolls' house from 1962 and a set of dolls' house furniture made
by German and Italian Prisoners of War during the Second
World War.

Whitby Museum
Pannett Park, Whitby, North Yorkshire YO21 1RE
Email: manager@whitbymuseum.org.uk
library@whitbymuseum.org.uk

www.whitbymuseum.org.uk
Large collection of toys includes a fully furnished dolls' house.

York Castle Museum
Eye of York, York YO1 9RY
Tel: 01904 687687
Email: enquiries@ymt.org.uk
www.yorkcastlemuseum.org.uk
Home to the Heslington baby house, dating from the early eighteenth century.

Scotland

The Hamilton Toy Museum and Collectors Shop
111 Main Street, Callander, Perthshire FK17 8BQ
Tel: 01877 330004
Email: info@thehamiltontoycollection.co.uk
https://thehamiltontoycollection.co.uk
Dolls' houses displayed in The Doll and Bear Room and in the Edwardian Nursery.

Highland Museum of Childhood
The Old Station, Strathpeffer IV14 9DH
Tel: 01997 421031
Email: info@highlandmuseumofchildhood.org.uk
www.highlandmuseumofchildhood.org.uk
Several dolls' houses included in the collection.

Little Treasures Toy Museum and Shop
Petersfield, Kemnay, Aberdeenshire AB51 5PR
Tel: 01467 641696
Email: emily@littlereasures.uk.com
www.littletreasures.uk.com/museum
Collection includes more than 350 dolls' houses and miniature displays, the largest collection of its kind in Scotland.

Museum of Childhood
42 High Street, Royal Mile, Edinburgh EH1 1TG
Tel: 0131 529 4142
Email: museumsandgalleries@edinburgh.gov.uk
www.edinburghmuseums.org.uk/Venues/Museum-of-Childhood
Collection includes several dolls' houses, shops, room settings
and other miniature items.

Scotland Street School Museum
Scotland Street, Glasgow G5 8QB
Tel: 01412 870500
Email: museums@glasgowlife.org.uk
www.glasgowlife.org.uk/museums/scotland-street/Pages/
default.aspx
Mackintosh-style 'Art Nouveau' model of Scotland Street School
on display, made by Brian Gallagher of BG Models Ltd for the
museum's 1996 Mackintosh exhibition.

The Lighthouse
11 Mitchell Lane, Glasgow G1 3NU
Tel: 01412 765365
Email: information.theLighthouse@glasgow.gov.uk
www.thelighthouse.co.uk
Mackintosh-style models of the Glasgow School of Art, Willow
Tea Rooms, Hill House and the Derngate in the Mackintosh
Centre.

Wales

Anglesey Model Village
Newborough, Llanfairpwllgwyngyll, Anglesey LL61 6RS
Tel: 01248 440488
Email: angleseymodelvillage@gmail.com
www.angleseymodelvillage.co.uk
Miniature recreations of Anglesey landmarks. Re-opened in
2019 after major refurbishment.

Erddig (National Trust)
Wrexham LL13 0YT

Tel: 01978 355314
Email: erddig@nationaltrust.org.uk
www.nationaltrust.org.uk/erddig
Dolls' house furniture from the nineteenth century.

Penrhyn Castle (National Trust)
Bangor, Gwynedd LL57 4HT
Tel: 01248 353084
penrhyncastle@nationaltrust.org.uk
www.nationaltrust.org.uk/penrhyn-castle
Four dolls' houses, including one Victorian, and extensive range
of furniture and other household objects on display.

West Wales Museum of Childhood
Pen-ffynnon, Llangeler, Carmarthenshire SA44 5EY
Tel: 01559 370428
Email: info@toymuseumwales.co.uk
www.toymuseumwales.co.uk
Large collection of mostly twentieth-century dolls' houses,
including Triang, Amersham, Handicrafts and others.

Northern Ireland

Springhill (National Trust)
20 Springhill Road, Moneymore, Mogherafelt, Co. Londonderry
BT45 7NQ
Tel: 028 8674 8210
Email: springhill@nationaltrust.org.uk
www.nationaltrust.org.uk/springhill
Small Victorian dolls' house.

Germany

Germanische Nationalmuseum
Kartausergasse 1, 90402 Nuremberg
Email: info@gnm.de
www.gnm.de
Dolls' houses from 16th and 17th centuries.

Schlossmuseum Arnstadt 'Neues Palais'
Schlossplatz 1, 99310 Arnstadt
Email: schlossmuseum@kultturbetrieb-arnstadt.de
www.kulturbetrieb-arnstadt.de
Mon Plaisir miniature town on display.

The Netherlands

Kunstmuseum Den Haag
Stadhouderslaan 41, 2517 HV Den Haag
(Postal address: PO Box 22, 2501 CB Den Haag)
Tel: +31 (0)70 338 1111
Email: info@kunstmuseum.nl
www.kunstmuseum.nl
Walnut cabinet house dating from 1743.

Rijksmuseum
Museumstraat 1, 1071 XX Amsterdam
(Postal address: Postbus 74888, 1070 DN Amsterdam)
Tel: +31 (0) 20 6747 000
Email: info@rijksmuseum.nl
www.rijksmuseum.nl
Two seventeenth century dolls' houses, including the one that
inspired Jessie Burton's novel *The Miniaturist*.

Centraal Museum Utrecht
Agnietenstraat 1, 3512 XA Utrecht
Tel: +31 (0) 30 236 2353
Email: info@centraalmuseum.nl
www.centraalmuseum.nl
Petronella de la Court's dolls' house from c1670.

Denmark

Egeskov Castle
Egeskov Gade 18, DK-5772 Kværndrup

Tel: +45 6227 1016
Email: info@egeskov.dk
www.egeskov.dk/en
Current home of Sir Nevile Wilkinson's Titania's Palace.

Dolls House Shops

The Dolls House
Market Place, Northleach, Cheltenham, Gloucester GL54 3EJ
Tel: 01451 860431
Email: sales@the-dollshouse.co.uk
www.the-dollshouse.co.uk

Dolls House Emporium
3 Cullet Drive, Queenborough, Kent ME11 5JS
Tel: 01795 665336
Email: support@dollshouse.com
www.dollshouse.com

Hobbies Ltd
Units 8B-11, The Raveningham Centre, Beccles Road,
Raveningham, Norwich,
Norfolk NR14 6NU
Tel: 01508 549330
Email: enquiries@alwayshobbies.com
www.alwayshobbies.com

Maple Street Dolls Houses and Miniatures
Maple Street, Wendy, Royston, Herts SG8 0AB
Tel: 01223 207025
Email: info@maplestreet.co.uk
www.maplestreet.co.uk

Dolls House Fairs and Festivals

Dolly Daydreams
www.dollysdaydreams.com

Little Priory Fairs
www.littleprioryfairs.co.uk

MGM Fairs
www.mgmfairs.co.uk

Miniatura
www.miniatura.co.uk

MM Fairs
www.dollshouse-fairs.co.uk

Kensington Dollshouse Festival (formerly the London Dollshouse
Festivals)
www.dollshousefestival.com

Warners Group
www.warnersgroup.co.uk/dolls-house-and-miniature-fairs

Wendy's World Fairs
www.wendysworldfairs.co.uk

Appendix 2

Further Reading

Although this is by no means an exhaustive list, dolls' house and model village enthusiasts of all ages should find something of interest here.

Books
History, collecting and making

Ackerman, Evelyn, *The Genius of Moritz Gottschalk: Blue and Red Roof Dollhouses, Stores, Kitchens, Stables and Other Miniature Structures* (Gold Horse, 1994)

Ali, Moi, *Dolls' Houses: A History and Collector's Guide* (Amberley Publishing, 2016)

Antrim, Liza, *Family Dolls' Houses of the eighteenth and nineteenth Centuries* (Cider House Books, 2011)

Boase, Tessa, *The Housekeeper's Tale* (Aurum Press, 2015)

Bristol, Olivia & Gedes-Brown, Leslie, *Dolls' Houses: Domestic life and architectural styles in miniature from the seventeenth century to the present day* (Mitchell Beazley, 1997)

Brown, Kenneth D., *The British Toy Industry* (Shire Publications, 2011)

Cadbury, Betty, *Playthings Past: A Collector's Guide to Antique Toys* (David & Charles, 1976)

Cole, Christopher, *Make Your Own Dolls' House* (Shepheard-Walwyn, 1976)

Constable, John, *Landscapes in Miniature* (Lutterworth Press, 1984)

Douet, Valerie Jackson, *Dolls' Houses: The Collector's Guide* (Magna Books, 1994)

Dunn, Tim, *Model Villages* (Amberley, 2017)

Earnshaw, Nora, *Collecting Dolls' Houses and Miniatures* (New Cavendish Books, 1999)

Eaton, Faith, *The Ultimate Dolls' House Book* (Dorling Kindersley, 1994)

Eaton Faith, *Classic Dolls' Houses* (Phoenix, 1997)

Forsyth, Hazel and Egan, Geoff, *Toys, Trinkets and Trifles: Base Metal Miniatures from London 1200 to 1800* (Unicorn Publishing Group, 2004)

Garfield, Simon, *In Miniature: How Small Things Illuminate the World* (Atria Books, 2019)

Greene, Vivien, *English Dolls' Houses of the Eighteenth and Nineteenth Centuries* (Bell & Hyman, 1955)

Greene, Vivien with Towner, Margaret, *The Vivien Greene Dolls' House Collection* (Cassell, 1995)

Hamilton, Caroline & Fiddick, Jane, *Our Dollshouses at Newby Hall, North Yorkshire* (Hudson's Media, 2015)

Hodgson, Mrs Willoughby, *The Quest of the Antique* (Herbert Jennnings Ltd, 1924)

Jacobs, Flora Gill, *A History of Doll Houses* (Bell & Hyman, 1965)

King, Constance Eileen, *Dolls and Dolls' Houses* (Bounty Books, 1996)

Lambton, Lucinda, *The Queen's Dolls' House* (Royal Collection Trust, 2010)

McCormack, Simon, *The Nostell Dolls' House* (National Trust, 2020)

Pasierbska, Halina, *Dolls' Houses* (Shire Publications Ltd, 2001)

Pasierbska, Halina, *Dolls' House Furniture* (Shire Publications Ltd, 2004)

Pasierbska, Halina, *Dolls' Houses from the V&A Museum of Childhood* (V&A Publishing, 2015)

Salter, Brian, *Model Towns and Villages* (In House Publications, 2014)

Wade, Charles Paget, *Days Far Away: Memories of Charles Paget Wade*, compiled and edited by Michael Jessup (National Trust Enterprises Ltd, 1996)

Fiction

A selection of adult's and children's plays, novels, stories and poetry inspired by dolls' houses and miniature worlds

Adults

Arlidge, M.J., *The Doll's House – A DI Helen Grace Thriller* (Penguin, 2015)

Burton, Jessie, *The Miniaturist* (Picador, 2014)

Dickens, Charles, *The Cricket on the Hearth* (Bradbury & Evans, 1845)

Hewson, David, *The House of Dolls* (Pan, 2014)

James, M.R., *The Haunted Dolls' House and Other Stories* (Penguin, 2008)

[Originally written in 1922 for Queen Mary's Dolls' House; first published in *Empire Review*, 16 March 1923]

Mansfield, Katherine, *The Doll's House* (Forgotten Books, April 2018)

[First published in political newspaper *The Nation and Atheneum* 4 February 1922; later published in *The Doves' Nest and Other Stories*, Constable, 1923]

Morgan, Phoebe, *The Doll House* (HQ/HarperCollins, 2018)

Phillips, Louise, *The Doll's House* (Hachette Books Ireland, 2014)

Price, Cate, *A Dollhouse to Die For* (Berkley Books, 2014)

Swift, Jonathan, *Gulliver's Travels* (Benjamin Motte, 1726)

Wells, H.G. *Tono-Bungay* (Macmillan, 1909)

Children and Young Adults

Carroll, Lewis, *Alice's Adventures in Wonderland* (Macmillan, 1865)

Dussling, Jennifer, *Eek! Stories to Make You Shriek: A Very Strange Doll's House* (Macmillan Children's Books, 1999)

Fine, Anne, *The Devil Walks* (Corgi, 2012)

Fisk, Nicholas, *The Model Village* (Walker Books, 1990)

Gardam, Jane, *Through the Dolls' House Door* (Walker Books, Ltd, 1989)

Godden, Rumer, *The Dolls' House* (Macmillan Children's Books, 2016)

[Originally published by Michael Joseph, 1947]

Hitchcock, Fleur, *Shrunk!* (Hot Key Books, 2012)

Jacobs, Flora Gill, *The Doll House Mystery* (Coward-McCann, 1958)

Johnson, Robyn, *The Enchanted Doll's House* (The Five Mile Press, 2005)

Norton, Mary, *The Borrowers Aloft* (Dent, 1961)

Potter, Beatrix, *A Tale of Two Bad Mice* (Warne & Co, 1904)

Ray, Jane, *The Dolls' House Fairy* (Orchard Books, 2010)

Unwin, Hilary, *Inside the Dollshouse – A Miniature Tale* (Shepheard-Walwyn Ltd, 1989)

[For adults and children]

Replicas of miniature books written exclusively for Queen Mary's Dolls' House Library

Miniature, cloth-bound editions, issued with booklet containing transcript of the story and information about the dolls' house.

Fougasse, *J. Smith* (Walker Books, 2015)

Holmes, Sherlock, *How Watson Learned the Trick* (Walker Books, 2014)

Story first published in *The Book of the Queen's Dolls' House Library* (Methuen, 1924) and in the *New York Times*, 24 August 1924.

Sackville-West, Vita, *A Note of Explanation* (Royal Collection Trust, 2017)

Magazines
Dolls House and Miniature Scene
Warners Group Publications, The Maltings, West Street, Bourne, Lincs PE10 9PH
www.dollshouseandminiaturescene.co.uk

Dolls House World
PO Box 2258, Pulborough RH20 9BA
www.dollshouseworld.com

Websites
Dolls Houses Past and Present
Comprehensive website devoted to all aspects of dolls' house history and collecting with articles, photographs, ezine, discussion forum and more.
www.dollshousespastandpresent.co.uk

Brighton Toy & Model Museum Index
www.brightontoymuseum.co.uk/index/main-page
Knowledge base for toys and models, general/social history. Regularly updated.

National Trust Collections
www.nationaltrustcollections.org.uk
Search the collections for dolls' houses and dolls' house furniture in the care of the National Trust.

Index